Praise from the SAS Community...

Longitudinal Data and SAS®: A Programmer's Guide, by Ron Cody, is a comprehensive look at the techniques to deal with longitudinal data—data that spans multiple observations. Ron's book looks at the problems encountered when working with longitudinal data, or in restructuring data into longitudinal data, and then examines techniques to solve each problem in detail. Some are very simple techniques, some are very novel techniques. Each is a useful addition to the basic knowledge that every SAS user should possess.

This is a very detailed book, with many examples to illustrate each idea and technique. It is an ideal book for the beginning SAS user. The discussions on fundamental data handling topics, and the insights into how SAS processes instructions like the LAG function, FIRST. and LAST., and the use of SAS procedures to deal with this type of data, are all highly useful and informative. More advanced SAS users will find much of the book's content is a refresher to knowledge they should already possess. However, every so often the user will encounter a little gem that will make this book a worthwhile addition to their SAS library, too. In general, I found *Longitudinal Data and SAS: A Programmer's Guide* to be an informative and thorough examination of the subject matter.

S. David Riba
JADE Tech, Inc.

Ron Cody is a SAS master and it shows in his ability to communicate through his writing. His book takes us step by step through the process of understanding and processing records in a vertical format. Ron guides us through the ways, from simple to complex, to view data and compare information from one time period to another. This book is user friendly and guides the beginner while challenging the advanced user. Through the use of the case study, Ron shows us data across several industries so that the audience can relate to data. Another good quality of the book is the introduction of the macros to make the processing of data an automatic one.

Janet Stuelpner
Steering Committee Member
Hartford Area SAS Users Group

Ron Cody has done an excellent job with this topic—longitudinal data. For some this description may seem strange or unfamiliar but it has to do with working with multiple records (observations) such as finding the mean (average) of a group of students' grades, number of patient visits, finding the first and last occurrence of a group of records, and much more.

The list of SAS data sets, programs, and macros are available from the SAS web site which will make following along in Ron's book very easy to duplicate his logs and to understand each and every step of his examples. The simplicity of data which Ron uses throughout his book makes it useable and understandable by most everyone in all industries.

Finally, Ron provides a number of solutions to his problems with a number of different approaches utilizing various techniques (a DATA step versus a PROC or arrays) that enlightens the new user to look at problems with varying viewpoints and creativity.

Charles Patridge
Corporate Actuarial Planning Unit
The Hartford

Longitudinal Data and SAS®

A PROGRAMMER'S GUIDE

RON CODY

The correct bibliographic citation for this manual is as follows: Cody, Ron. 2001. *Longitudinal Data and SAS®: A Programmer's Guide,* Cary, NC: SAS Institute Inc.

Longitudinal Data and SAS®: A Programmer's Guide

SAS Institute Inc., SAS Campus Drive, Cary, North Carolina 27513.

1st printing, November 2001
2nd printing, February 2005
3rd printing, June 2007
4th printing, December 2008

SAS® Publishing provides a complete selection of books and electronic products to help customers use SAS software to its fullest potential. For more information about our e-books, e-learning products, CDs, and hard-copy books, visit the SAS Publishing Web site at **support.sas.com/publishing** or call 1-800-727-3228.

Table of Contents

1 The RETAIN Statement

2 The LAG and DIF Functions

3 FIRST. and LAST. Temporary Variables

Flags and Counters

Summarizing Data Using PROC MEANS and PROC FREQ

6 Using PROC SQL with Longitudinal Data

7 Restructuring SAS Data Sets Using Arrays

8 Restructuring SAS Data Sets Using PROC TRANSPOSE

9 Study One: Operations on a Clinical Database

10 Study Two: Operations on Daily Weather Data and Ozone Levels

11 Study Three: Producing Summary Reports on a Library Data Set

12 Useful Macros

Appendix List of Data Files and SAS Data Sets

Index

List of Programs

1 The RETAIN Statement

2 The LAG and DIF Functions

3 FIRST. and LAST. Temporary Variables

4   Flags and Counters

5   Summarizing Data Using PROC MEANS and PROC FREQ

6 Using PROC SQL with Longitudinal Data

7 Restructuring SAS Data Sets Using Arrays

8   Restructuring SAS Data Sets Using PROC TRANSPOSE

9 Study One: Operations on a Clinical Database

10 Study Two: Operations on Daily Weather Data and Ozone Levels

11 Study Three: Producing Summary Reports on a Library Data Set

12 Useful Macros

Appendix List of Data Files and SAS Data Sets

Preface

In a SAS data set, performing calculations within an observation is relatively simple; performing calculations or making comparisons between observations is more difficult. In this book I use the term longitudinal data techniques to refer to operations involving two or more observations per subject. For example, a SAS data set of clinical data may contain a separate observation for each patient visit. Thus, the number of observations per patient could differ among patients. SAS software provides many powerful tools such as the LAG function, FIRST. and LAST. logical variables, or variables whose values are retained, for making calculations between observations. It is also easier to look backward rather than look ahead. For example, the LAG function can give you access to a value from previous observations, but there is no comparable function that looks ahead. In this book, you will learn a technique for looking ahead across observations.

This book covers SAS programming techniques for conducting operations between observations in a SAS data set. Programs in this book were run using SAS Release 8.2, although many of the programs can be run using versions prior to Version 7 (you might have to shorten some variable names). Statistical techniques commonly used with these types of data, such as survival analysis or time series techniques, are not covered. This is primarily a book about SAS programming.

Chapters 1 through 8 introduce many of the SAS programming techniques that are useful when handling longitudinal data. Through carefully developed examples, you will understand the inner workings of the SAS DATA step, how and when variables are initialized, what happens when a variable is retained, exactly how the LAG function works, and many other SAS programming techniques. SAS procedures such as MEANS and FREQ are useful for summarizing multiple observations per subject. Finally, restructuring a SAS data set by using a DATA step or PROC TRANSPOSE is yet another technique for performing calculations between observations.

In Chapters 9 through 11, examples of longitudinal data techniques, taken from several different fields, are offered. You will see how to extract the first or last observation for a subject; how to compute differences between successive observations or between the first and last observation for a subject; how to compute the mean, median, minimum, or maximum value of a variable across multiple observations. You will see how to compute a moving average using a data set containing daily ozone, pollen, and various other measurements.

Finally, Chapter 12 contains some useful macros for processing longitudinal data. You can easily download and modify the macros, as well as all of the code from this book, from the companion Web site at www.sas.com/companionsites. In addition to a link to the example code, the companion Web site also features sample chapters, additional resources, and updates.

Acknowledgments

I don't really know how many people read the acknowledgments, but to me, they are a very important part of the book. Here I get to thank the people who helped make this book possible. Although it is my name that gets all the "glory" on the cover, I received lots of help. First of all, I want to thank Judy Whatley, who was the acquisitions editor for this book. I have worked with Judy before, and it is always a pleasure. It's nice to know there is someone who actually knows all the rules of writing who is looking over my work before it is released. Next, I want to thank the five reviewers, George Berg, Paul Grant, Kevin Hobbs, Peter Welbrock, and Mike Zdeb, who made numerous suggestions to improve the book.

The editing and production of the book were accomplished by the hard work of Tate Renner, copyeditor; Candy Farrell, technical publishing specialist; Cate Parrish, designer; and Patricia Spain and Ericka Wilcher, marketing analysts. Thank you all.

Ron Cody
Summer 2001

xx

1

The RETAIN Statement

Introduction

Suppose you have a SAS data set of clinical data. Each observation corresponds to a visit to the clinic and contains such information as a patient number, the date of the visit, and some information about the visit. It would be useful to compare information from one visit to another, for a given patient. How many days were there from the previous visit? Did this patient's blood pressure go up or down? Questions such as these are traditionally more difficult to answer using SAS software than comparisons within an observation. This first chapter introduces one of the most useful tools for "remembering" information from a previous observation—the RETAIN statement. You will see, in detail, exactly how this versatile statement works and how to avoid getting in trouble when using it.

Demonstrating a DATA Step with and without a RETAIN Statement

The RETAIN statement is often a mystery to beginning SAS programmers. To understand how the RETAIN statement works, you must first understand the basic operation of the SAS DATA step.

Program 1-1 demonstrates a SAS DATA step where a RETAIN statement is not used.

Program 1-1: Demonstrating a DATA Step without a RETAIN Statement

```
DATA WITHOUT_1;
   PUT "Before the INPUT statement:   " _ALL_ ;   ❶
   INPUT X @@;
   PUT "After the INPUT statement:    " _ALL_ /;
DATALINES;
1 2 . 3
;
```

By placing the PUT statements at strategic places in the DATA step, you can see what is going on "behind the scenes." A PUT statement writes out text or the value of variables to the location specified by a FILE statement. Since there is no FILE statement in this DATA step, the results of the PUT statements are written to the SAS Log (the default location). The keyword _ALL_ ❶ causes the PUT statement to output the value of all the variables, including some SAS internal variables, such as _N_.

Before we examine the log produced by this program, let's be sure that you understand the meaning of the double @ sign in the INPUT statement. A trailing double @ says to the DATA step, "Hold the line." That is, do not move the pointer to a new line each time the DATA step iterates. Instead, just keep on reading data values until there are no more on the line. Many of the examples in this book will use a trailing double @ to save some space and make the programs more compact (and perhaps easier to read).

Let's look at the SAS log that results from running Program 1-1:

```
78    DATA WITHOUT_1;
79       PUT "Before the INPUT statement:   " _ALL_;
80       INPUT X @@;
81       PUT "After the INPUT statement:    " _ALL_ /;
82    DATALINES;

Before the INPUT statement:   X=. _ERROR_=0 _N_=1
After the INPUT statement:    X=1 _ERROR_=0 _N_=1

Before the INPUT statement:   X=. _ERROR_=0 _N_=2
After the INPUT statement:    X=2 _ERROR_=0 _N_=2

Before the INPUT statement:   X=. _ERROR_=0 _N_=3
After the INPUT statement:    X=. _ERROR_=0 _N_=3

Before the INPUT statement:   X=. _ERROR_=0 _N_=4
After the INPUT statement:    X=3 _ERROR_=0 _N_=4

Before the INPUT statement:   X=. _ERROR_=0 _N_=5
```

Notice that the value of X is a missing value at the top of the DATA step (before the INPUT statement). This is the usual way that a SAS DATA step operates. Notice also that the DATA step does not stop until it tries to read a fifth data value and realizes that there are no more data values to read.

Let's modify Program 1-1 by adding a RETAIN statement.

Program 1-2: Demonstrating a DATA Step with a RETAIN Statement

```
DATA WITH_1;
   RETAIN X;
   PUT "Before the INPUT statement:   " _ALL_;
   INPUT X @@;
   PUT "After the INPUT statement:    " _ALL_ /;
DATALINES;
1 2 . 3
;
```

The resulting log is shown next:

```
86    DATA WITH_1;
87       RETAIN X;
88       PUT "Before the INPUT statement:   " _ALL_;
89       INPUT X @@;
90       PUT "After the INPUT statement:    " _ALL_ /;
91    DATALINES;

Before the INPUT statement:   X=. _ERROR_=0 _N_=1
After the INPUT statement:    X=1 _ERROR_=0 _N_=1

Before the INPUT statement:   X=1 _ERROR_=0 _N_=2
After the INPUT statement:    X=2 _ERROR_=0 _N_=2

Before the INPUT statement:   X=2 _ERROR_=0 _N_=3
After the INPUT statement:    X=. _ERROR_=0 _N_=3

Before the INPUT statement:   X=. _ERROR_=0 _N_=4
After the INPUT statement:    X=3 _ERROR_=0 _N_=4

Before the INPUT statement:   X=3 _ERROR_=0 _N_=5
```

Notice that the value of X is missing the first time, but for each additional iteration of the DATA step, it retains the value it had in the previous iteration. Notice that the value of X is missing after the third value of X is read. This missing value is retained just as all the other nonmissing values in this example.

In its simplest form, a RETAIN statement takes the form RETAIN *list_of_variables*; by the way, it doesn't matter where we place the RETAIN statement in the DATA step—the effect is the same.

There was no reason to use a RETAIN statement in Program 1-2 other than to demonstrate how a DATA step runs with and without such a statement. The next example, Program 1-3, is an attempt (that does not work) to use a value from a previous observation whenever a missing value is read from the input data.

Program 1-3: Demonstrating a DATA Step That Does Not Work without a RETAIN Statement

```
***If there is a missing value for X, use the value
   from the previous observation ;
***Note: This program does NOT work as planned;
DATA WITHOUT_2;
   PUT "Before INPUT:      " _ALL_ ;
   INPUT X @@;
   IF X NE . THEN OLD_X = X;
   ELSE X = OLD_X;
   PUT "After assignment:  " _ALL_ /;
DATALINES;
1 2 . 3
;
```

The goal of this program is to substitute a value of X for a previous nonmissing value of X whenever the current value of X (read from the input data) is a missing value. However, as we can see in the log below, this program does not work because OLD_X is set to a missing value at the top of the DATA step for every iteration.

```
94    ***If there is a missing value for X, use the value
95       from the previous observation ;
96    ***Note: This program does NOT work as planned;
97    DATA WITHOUT_2;
98       PUT "Before INPUT:      " _ALL_ ;
99       INPUT X @@;
100      IF X NE . THEN OLD_X = X;
101      ELSE X = OLD_X;
102      PUT "After assignment:  " _ALL_ /;
103   DATALINES;

Before INPUT:      X=. OLD_X=. _ERROR_=0 _N_=1
After assignment:  X=1 OLD_X=1 _ERROR_=0 _N_=1
Before INPUT:      X=. OLD_X=. _ERROR_=0 _N_=2
After assignment:  X=2 OLD_X=2 _ERROR_=0 _N_=2

Before INPUT:      X=. OLD_X=. _ERROR_=0 _N_=3
After assignment:  X=. OLD_X=. _ERROR_=0 _N_=3

Before INPUT:      X=. OLD_X=. _ERROR_=0 _N_=4
After assignment:  X=3 OLD_X=3 _ERROR_=0 _N_=4

Before INPUT:      X=. OLD_X=. _ERROR_=0 _N_=5
```

You can see that OLD_X is assigned the nonmissing values as planned, but the PUT statement right after the DATA statement shows that it is set to missing each time the DATA step iterates and the program fails to work as desired.

Look at Program 1-4 to see how a RETAIN statement changes things.

Program 1-4: Adding a RETAIN Statement to Program 1-3

```
***If there is a missing value for X, use the value
   from the previous observation;
***Note: With the added RETAIN statement, the program now works;
DATA WITH_2;
   RETAIN OLD_X;
   PUT "Before INPUT:        " _ALL_ ;
   INPUT X @@;
   IF X NE . THEN OLD_X = X;
   ELSE X = OLD_X;
   PUT "After assignment:  " _ALL_ /;
DATALINES;
1 2 . 3
;
```

This is the resulting output:

```
106   ***If there is a missing value for X, use the value
107      from the previous observation;
108   ***Note: With the added RETAIN statement, the program now works;
109   DATA WITH_2;
110      RETAIN OLD_X;
111      PUT "Before INPUT:        " _ALL_ ;
112      INPUT X @@;
113      IF X NE . THEN OLD_X = X;
114      ELSE X = OLD_X;
115      PUT "After assignment:  " _ALL_ /;
116   DATALINES;

Before INPUT:        OLD_X=. X=. _ERROR_=0 _N_=1
After assignment:  OLD_X=1 X=1 _ERROR_=0 _N_=1

Before INPUT:        OLD_X=1 X=. _ERROR_=0 _N_=2
After assignment:  OLD_X=2 X=2 _ERROR_=0 _N_=2

Before INPUT:        OLD_X=2 X=. _ERROR_=0 _N_=3
After assignment:  OLD_X=2 X=2 _ERROR_=0 _N_=3

Before INPUT:        OLD_X=2 X=. _ERROR_=0 _N_=4
After assignment:  OLD_X=3 X=3 _ERROR_=0 _N_=4

Before INPUT:        OLD_X=3 X=. _ERROR_=0 _N_=5
```

Notice that the variable OLD_X holds on to the value from the previous iteration of the DATA step, and when X is missing (the third data value), the previous X value (2) is substituted for the missing value.

Generating Sequential SUBJECT Numbers Using a Retained Variable

Let's look at a very common programming requirement: adding sequential SUBJECT numbers to a set of data. As we did before, the first attempt will be without a RETAIN statement to demonstrate why a RETAIN statement is needed.

Program 1-5: Attempting to Generate a Sequential SUBJECT Number without Using a RETAIN Statement

```
***Attempting to generate a sequential SUBJECT number without
   using a RETAIN statement;
DATA WITHOUT_3;
   PUT "Before the INPUT statement: " _ALL_ ;
   INPUT X @@;
   SUBJECT = SUBJECT + 1;   ❶
   PUT "After the INPUT statement: " _ALL_ /;
DATALINES;
1 3 5
;
```

The programmer is trying to generate a subject number in line ❶. Before any data values (X's) have been read, SUBJECT (and X) are both set to missing. Therefore, when you attempt to add 1 to a missing value, the result is a missing value. The log below shows that SUBJECT is missing in every observation:

```
119   ***Attempting to generate a sequential SUBJECT number without
120      using an assignment statement;
121   DATA WITHOUT_3;
122      PUT "Before the INPUT statement: " _ALL_ ;
123      INPUT X @@;
124      SUBJECT = SUBJECT + 1;
125      PUT "After the INPUT statement: " _ALL_ /;
126   DATALINES;

Before the INPUT statement: X=. SUBJECT=. _ERROR_=0 _N_=1
After the INPUT statement: X=1 SUBJECT=. _ERROR_=0 _N_=1

Before the INPUT statement: X=. SUBJECT=. _ERROR_=0 _N_=2
After the INPUT statement: X=3 SUBJECT=. _ERROR_=0 _N_=2

Before the INPUT statement: X=. SUBJECT=. _ERROR_=0 _N_=3
After the INPUT statement: X=5 SUBJECT=. _ERROR_=0 _N_=3

Before the INPUT statement: X=. SUBJECT=. _ERROR_=0 _N_=4
```

A RETAIN statement will fix this problem. Besides retaining the value of SUBJECT, you need to supply an initial value as well. This is done in the RETAIN statement. If you follow the variable name with a number, the value of the retained variable will be initialized to that number. That is, it will continue to be the initialized value until it is replaced by another value. Program 1-6 shows the corrected version of this program with the RETAIN statement added.

Program 1-6: Adding a RETAIN Statement to Program 1-5

```
***The same program with a RETAIN statement;
DATA WITH_3;
    RETAIN SUBJECT 0;   ❶
    PUT "Before the INPUT statement: " _ALL_ ;
    INPUT X @@;
    SUBJECT = SUBJECT + 1;   ❷
    PUT "After the INPUT statement: " _ALL_ /;
DATALINES;
1 3 5
;
```

Notice that SUBJECT is retained and the initial value is set to 0 (line ❶). Therefore, the first time line ❷ is executed, you are adding $0 + 1 = 1$ and assigning this value to SUBJECT. Since SUBJECT is retained, the next time line ❷ executes, you will be adding 1 to the previous value

(1) and SUBJECT will have a value of 2, and so forth. To be certain this is clear, you can inspect the log below:

```
131    *The same program with a RETAIN statement;
132    DATA WITH_3;
133       RETAIN SUBJECT 0;
134       PUT "Before the INPUT statement: " _ALL_ ;
135       INPUT X @@;
136       SUBJECT = SUBJECT + 1;
137       PUT "After the INPUT statement: " _ALL_ /;
138    DATALINES;

Before the INPUT statement: SUBJECT=0 X=. _ERROR_=0 _N_=1
After the INPUT statement: SUBJECT=1 X=1 _ERROR_=0 _N_=1

Before the INPUT statement: SUBJECT=1 X=. _ERROR_=0 _N_=2
After the INPUT statement: SUBJECT=2 X=3 _ERROR_=0 _N_=2

Before the INPUT statement: SUBJECT=2 X=. _ERROR_=0 _N_=3
After the INPUT statement: SUBJECT=3 X=5 _ERROR_=0 _N_=3

Before the INPUT statement: SUBJECT=3 X=. _ERROR_=0 _N_=4
```

The program is now working as planned.

Using a SUM Statement to Create SUBJECT Numbers

Creating SUBJECT numbers or other counters in a SAS DATA step is such a common operation, the thoughtful folks at SAS came up with a special SUM statement that makes this process easier. Look at Program 1-7, which uses a SUM statement to accomplish the same objective as Program 1-6.

Program 1-7: Demonstrating the SUM Statement

```
DATA WITHOUT_4;
   PUT "Before the INPUT statement: " _ALL_ ;
   INPUT X @@;
   SUBJECT + 1;  /* SUM statement */  ❶
   PUT "After the INPUT statement: " _ALL_ /;
DATALINES;
1 3 5
;
```

Line ❶ is a SUM statement. This is a funny-looking statement to people used to programming in other languages, because there is no equal sign. That is what makes this a SUM statement rather than an assignment statement. It accomplishes several objectives. It automatically retains the variable in the statement (SUBJECT here) and sets the initial value to 0. Inspection of the log below shows that it works as designed:

```
155   DATA WITHOUT_4;
156      PUT "Before the INPUT statement: " _ALL_ ;
157      INPUT X @@;
158      SUBJECT + 1;   /* SUM statement */
159      PUT "After the INPUT statement: " _ALL_ /;
160   DATALINES;

Before the INPUT statement: X=. SUBJECT=0 _ERROR_=0 _N_=1
After the INPUT statement: X=1 SUBJECT=1 _ERROR_=0 _N_=1

Before the INPUT statement: X=. SUBJECT=1 _ERROR_=0 _N_=2
After the INPUT statement: X=3 SUBJECT=2 _ERROR_=0 _N_=2

Before the INPUT statement: X=. SUBJECT=2 _ERROR_=0 _N_=3
After the INPUT statement: X=5 SUBJECT=3 _ERROR_=0 _N_=3

Before the INPUT statement: X=. SUBJECT=3 _ERROR_=0 _N_=4
```

Demonstrating That Variables Read with a SET Statement Are Retained

There is another way in which SAS implicitly retains variables. Variables read with a SET statement are automatically retained. Most of the time, we don't really need to think about this. However, there are times when this feature of the SET statement can be used to our advantage. The small demonstration program shown next creates a data set with one observation (X=1 and Y=2). In the DATA step that follows, a SET statement is conditionally executed. Look at Program 1-8 and the resulting log.

Program 1-8: Demonstrating That Variables from a SET Statement Are Retained

```
DATA ONE;
   INPUT X Y;
DATALINES;
1 2
;
```

```
DATA TWO;
   IF _N_ = 1 THEN SET ONE;
   PUT "Before INPUT statement: " _ALL_;
   INPUT NEW;
   PUT "After INPUT statement: " _ALL_ / ;
DATALINES;
3
4
5
;
```

Here is the SAS log from running this program:

```
171   DATA TWO;
172      IF _N_ = 1 THEN SET ONE;
173      PUT "Before INPUT statement: " _ALL_;
174      INPUT NEW;
175      PUT "After INPUT statement: " _ALL_ / ;
176   DATALINES;

Before INPUT statement: X=1 Y=2 NEW=. _ERROR_=0 _N_=1
After INPUT statement: X=1 Y=2 NEW=3 _ERROR_=0 _N_=1

Before INPUT statement: X=1 Y=2 NEW=. _ERROR_=0 _N_=2
After INPUT statement: X=1 Y=2 NEW=4 _ERROR_=0 _N_=2

Before INPUT statement: X=1 Y=2 NEW=. _ERROR_=0 _N_=3
After INPUT statement: X=1 Y=2 NEW=5 _ERROR_=0 _N_=3

Before INPUT statement:  X=1 Y=2 NEW=. _ERROR_=0 _N_=4
```

Notice that the values of X and Y remain at 1 and 2, respectively, in every observation in the data set TWO. Without the implicit retain feature of the SET statement, this would not work.

A Caution When Using a RETAIN Statement

There are some serious pitfalls that you can encounter when using the RETAIN statement. For example, suppose you want to read several observations from one SAS data set and create a single observation in a new data set. Under certain circumstances where you have missing values and you are using retained variables, you may make the mistake of using a retained value from a previous subject instead of a missing value for the present subject. We will demonstrate and discuss an example later in this book (see Program 7-7). So think of the RETAIN statement when you need to "remember" information from previous observations, but be especially cautious and test your programs carefully.

2 The LAG and DIF Functions

Introduction

When you think about looking back across observations, you either think about using retained variables or the LAG function. Retained variables allow you to access values of SAS variables from previous observations. The LAG functions (LAG, LAG2, and so forth) are more specific: they return values from previous iterations of the DATA step. One common application for a LAG function is to compare a value in the current observation to one in the previous observation. This provides you with an easy way to compute differences between observations in a SAS data set. This chapter describes how LAG and DIF functions work. The true actions of these functions are not always understood, even by programmers who have been using them for years.

Using the LAG Function to Compute Differences

The true definition of the LAG function is that it returns the value of its argument the last time the same LAG function executed. This function is often, mistakenly, thought of as a function that returns the value of a variable from a previous observation. While this is sometimes true, several examples in this chapter will show why this is not always true.

Program 2-1 demonstrates how to use the LAG function to compare values between observations.

Program 2-1: Using the LAG Function to Compare a Value in the Current Observation to One in the Previous Observation

```
DATA COMPARE;
   INPUT X;
   LAST_X = LAG(X);    ❶
   DIFF_X = X - LAST_X;   ❷
DATALINES;
4
2
9
6
;
PROC PRINT DATA=COMPARE NOOBS;
   TITLE "Demonstrating the LAG Function";
RUN;
```

The first value of X is 4. Since this is the first time the LAG function has executed (line ❶), the value of LAST_X is missing. Since LAST_X is missing, DIFF_X ❷ will also be missing. When the DATA step iterates for the second time, X is equal to 2 and LAG(X) is the value of X the last time this LAG function executed: 4. Therefore, LAST_X is equal to 4 and DIFF_X is equal to −2. This continues until all the data values have been read. When the LAG function is executed for *every iteration of the DATA step*, you can think of the function as returning a value from the previous observation. Look at the listing below to confirm that this program is working as designed:

```
Demonstrating the LAG Function

X      LAST_X    DIFF_X

4         .         .
2         4        -2
9         2         7
6         9        -3
```

Why are we making such a fuss about the subtle differences between the true definition of the LAG function and the simpler interpretation that it returns the value from the previous observation? Because ignoring this subtle difference can get you in trouble as demonstrated in Program 2-2.

Program 2-2: Demonstrating What Happens When You Execute the LAG Function Conditionally

```
DATA LAG2;
   INPUT X;
   IF X > 2 THEN LAG_X = LAG(X);
DATALINES;
1
3
.
5
2
7
;
PROC PRINT DATA=LAG2;
   TITLE "Listing of LAG1 Data Set";
RUN;
```

Can you predict the values of LAG_X for each of the six observations in the data set LAG2? The answer is

```
Listing of LAG1 Data Set

Obs    X    LAG_X

 1     1      .
 2     3      .
 3     .      .
 4     5      3
 5     2      .
 6     7      5
```

What's happening here? The first time the LAG function executes is the second observation where X is equal to 3. The next time the LAG function executes is in the fourth observation where X is equal to 5. The value of LAG_X is the value of X the last time the function executed, which was when X was equal to 3. Therefore, the value of LAG_X in the fourth observation is 3. In the last observation, X is equal to 7, the IF statement is true, and the LAG function returns a 5, which is the value of X the last time the LAG function executed. It is tempting to say never execute the LAG function conditionally, but you will see a program later in this book that does just that—and it does just what it is supposed to do!

Demonstrating Some Related Functions: LAG2, LAG3, and So Forth

Besides the LAG function, there is a family of functions: LAG2, LAG3, etc. As you might expect, the LAG2 function returns the value from two previous executions of the function; LAG3, three previous executions, and so forth. Program 2-3 should make this clear.

Program 2-3: Demonstrating the LAG*n* Functions

```
DATA LAG_N;
   INPUT X;
   LAG_X = LAG(X);
   LAG2_X = LAG2(X);
   LAG3_X = LAG3(X);
DATALINES;
1
2
3
4
5
;
PROC PRINT DATA=LAG_N;
   TITLE "Demonstrating the LAGn Family of Functions";
RUN;
```

Here is the output:

```
Demonstrating the LAGn Family of Functions

Obs    X     LAG_X     LAG2_X     LAG3_X

 1     1       .          .          .
 2     2       1          .          .
 3     3       2          1          .
 4     4       3          2          1
 5     5       4          3          2
```

As a very useful "mental crutch" you can think of the LAG*n* function as producing values of a variable from a previous *n*th observation, but only if you execute it for every iteration of the DATA step. Looking at the output above, you see that the value of LAG3_X is missing for the first three observations, and from then on it is equal to the value of X going back three observations.

Demonstrating the DIF Function

Since the LAG function is often used to compute the difference between the value of the current observation and a previous observation, for those of you who are typing-challenged, you can save a few key strokes and use the DIF function, which is defined as

```
DIF(X) = X - LAG(X)
```

There is also a family of DIF*n* functions related to the family of LAG*n* functions. (**Note:** Although related, these two families seem to differ on everything!)

To demonstrate the DIF function, here is Program 2-1, rewritten to use the DIF function.

Program 2-4: Rewriting Program 2-1 to Use the DIF Function

```
DATA COMPARE;
   INPUT X;
   DIFF_X = DIF(X);
DATALINES;
4
2
9
6
;
PROC PRINT DATA=COMPARE NOOBS;
   TITLE "Demonstrating the DIF Function";
RUN;
```

The values of DIFF_X are identical to the values produced by Program 2-1.

The take-home message is to remember the LAG function when you want to compare a value in the current observation to a value from an earlier observation, as long as you want to look back a fixed number of observations. Now that you have seen the RETAIN statement and the LAG function, you realize that there will be times when either of them can be used. The RETAIN statement is probably the more flexible of the two since it can "remember" the value of a variable from any previous observation. The LAG function may be simpler to use but is only useful when you want to look back a fixed number of observations.

3 FIRST. and LAST. Temporary Variables

Introduction

Let's use the scenario of a clinical data set again, as a way of describing one common application of FIRST. and LAST. variables. You have a data set of patient visits to a clinic where each patient may have one or more visits (each visit being an observation). If you had an easy way to determine when you were reading the first observation (or the last observation) for each patient, you could use this information to count the number of visits for each patient or to determine if a given patient came in more than once for the same problem. FIRST. and LAST. temporary variables provide a convenient way of knowing when you are reading the first or last observation for a subject or for some other grouping variable. To learn how to use these variables, read on.

When you have multiple observations per subject or some other grouping variable (also called a BY variable in SAS terminology), with one magic statement, you can create two temporary SAS variables that will allow you to know when you are reading the first or the last observation for that subject (or other grouping variable). This immensely powerful tool is referred to as FIRST. (pronounced "first dot") and LAST. temporary (sometimes called logical) variables.

How to Create FIRST. and LAST. Temporary Variables

To see how you create these temporary variables, let's first create a small test data set that contains two variables, SUBJECT and SCORE, by running Program 3-1.

Program 3-1: Creating a Test Data Set

```
***Demonstrating FIRST. and LAST. temporary variables;
DATA ONE;
   INPUT SUBJECT SCORE;
DATALINES;
1 11
2 21
3 31
1 12
4 41
1 13
2 22
4 42
4 43
;
```

In order to create FIRST. and LAST. temporary variables, if the data set is not already sorted, you must first sort the data set by the grouping variable(s).

```
PROC SORT DATA=ONE;
   BY SUBJECT;
RUN;
```

A listing of the sorted data set is shown below:

```
Listing of Data Set ONE

Obs      SUBJECT      SCORE

 1          1          11
 2          1          12
 3          1          13
 4          2          21
 5          2          22
 6          3          31
 7          4          41
 8          4          42
 9          4          43
```

The next step is to create a new SAS data set from the sorted data set by using a SET statement. Following the SET statement with a BY statement creates the temporary variables. Look at Program 3-2 and the explanation that follows.

Program 3-2: Creating the FIRST. and LAST. Temporary Variables

```
DATA TWO;
   SET ONE;     ❶
   BY SUBJECT;     ❷
   FIRST = FIRST.SUBJECT;     ❸
   LAST = LAST.SUBJECT;     ❹
RUN;

PROC PRINT DATA=TWO;
   TITLE "Demonstrating FIRST. and LAST. Variables";
RUN;
```

As we mentioned above, you must be sure the data set is sorted by the grouping variable (SUBJECT, in this case). The SET statement ❶ makes a copy of the data set ONE, and the BY statement ❷ causes the two variables FIRST.SUBJECT and LAST.SUBJECT to be created. These variables have only two values, 0 or 1. Zero can also be thought of as "false" and 1 as "true." That is, if you are processing the first observation for a SUBJECT, FIRST.SUBJECT will be 1 (true). If you are not processing the first observation for a SUBJECT, the value of FIRST.SUBJECT will be 0 (false). Normally, you would want to use these temporary variables in data set TWO to do something useful. Here, nothing useful is being done with these variables. This is only a demonstration of how to create them.

These variables are temporary and do not appear in data set TWO. They are used by the programmer in the DATA step. For each variable in the BY statement, there will be corresponding FIRST. and LAST. temporary variables. You will see later in this chapter what happens when there is more than one BY variable. For demonstration purposes only, lines ❸ and ❹ were added to Program 3-2. This way, you can see the value of the temporary variables for every observation in the data set TWO. Here is the output from the PROC PRINT:

```
Demonstrating FIRST. and LAST. Variables

Obs     SUBJECT     SCORE     FIRST     LAST

 1         1          11         1         0
 2         1          12         0         0
 3         1          13         0         1
 4         2          21         1         0
 5         2          22         0         1
 6         3          31         1         1
 7         4          41         1         0
 8         4          42         0         0
 9         4          43         0         1
```

Just as you might expect, the variable FIRST, which was set equal to the temporary variable FIRST.SUBJECT, is equal to 1 (true) for the first observation for each SUBJECT and equal to 0 (false) for every other observation. In a similar manner, the variable LAST, equal to the temporary variable LAST.SUBJECT, is equal to 1 (true) in the last observation for each SUBJECT and 0 otherwise. Notice that both FIRST.SUBJECT and LAST.SUBJECT are equal to 1 (true) for subject number 3. Why? Because there is only one observation for this subject, making it both the first and the last observation for this subject. Knowing when you are processing the first or last observation for a subject or other grouping variable can be very useful when working with longitudinal data.

Using More Than One BY Variable

What happens when there is more than one BY variable? Program 3-3 demonstrates this situation.

Program 3-3: Creating FIRST. and LAST. Variables When There Is More Than One BY Variable

```
DATA THREE;
    INFORMAT GENDER GROUP $1.;
    INPUT GENDER GROUP SCORE;
DATALINES;
M A 23
M A 24
M B 33
M B 35
M B 36
F A 41
F A 42
F A 43
F B 51
;
PROC SORT DATA=THREE;    ❶
   BY GENDER GROUP;
RUN;

DATA FOUR;
   SET THREE;
   BY GENDER GROUP;    ❷
   ***Create variables to demonstrate how the FIRST.
      and LAST. variables work with two BY variables;
   FIRST_GENDER = FIRST.GENDER;    ❸
```

```
   LAST_GENDER = LAST.GENDER;    ❹
   FIRST_GROUP = FIRST.GROUP;    ❺
   LAST_GROUP = LAST.GROUP;      ❻

PROC PRINT DATA=FOUR;
   TITLE "Listing of Data Set FOUR";
RUN;
```

This program is similar to Program 3-2, except that there are two BY variables instead of one. Again, you must be sure the data set is sorted by each of the variables for which you want to create FIRST. and LAST. variables ❶. Next, you follow the SET statement with the BY statement ❷. That's all there is to it. For demonstration purposes only, this program creates four real variables equal to the four temporary variables so you can see the results in the PROC PRINT that follows.

```
Listing of Data Set FOUR

                                  FIRST_     LAST_     FIRST_     LAST_
Obs    GENDER    GROUP    SCORE   GENDER     GENDER    GROUP      GROUP

 1       F         A       41       1          0         1          0
 2       F         A       42       0          0         0          0
 3       F         A       43       0          0         0          1
 4       F         B       51       0          1         1          1
 5       M         A       23       1          0         1          0
 6       M         A       24       0          0         0          1
 7       M         B       33       0          0         1          0
 8       M         B       35       0          0         0          0
 9       M         B       36       0          1         0          1
```

The value of the four FIRST. and LAST. variables are obvious for the first observation. Things get a bit trickier in observation four. GENDER is still equal to "F" so FIRST_GENDER is still 0. However, GROUP has changed from "A" to "B," so FIRST_GROUP is equal to 1 (true). It is important to recognize the sort order when interpreting the FIRST. and LAST. temporary variables. The FIRST. BY variable is true whenever its value has changed from the previous observation.

A Simple Application Using FIRST. and LAST. Variables

In the case studies in Chapters 9–11, you will see many uses for the temporary variables described in this chapter. However, before leaving this section, it would be useful to see one common use of these variables. The program shown next uses temporary variables to count the number of scores for each SUBJECT in the data set ONE (created by Program 3-1).

Program 3-4: Using FIRST. and LAST. Variables to Count Observations per Subject

```
PROC SORT DATA=ONE;
   BY SUBJECT;
RUN;

DATA COUNT;
   SET ONE;
   BY SUBJECT;

   IF FIRST.SUBJECT = 1 THEN NUMBER = 0;   ❶
   NUMBER + 1;   ❷

   IF LAST.SUBJECT = 1 THEN OUTPUT;   ❸
   KEEP SUBJECT NUMBER;
RUN;

PROC PRINT DATA=COUNT;
   TITLE "Counting Observations per Subject";
RUN;
```

Each time you encounter a new subject (FIRST.SUBJECT is true), you set your count variable (NUMBER, in this example) to 0 (line ❶). In computerese this is called *initialization*.

Note that since FIRST.SUBJECT is a logical variable, line ❶ can also be written like this:

```
IF FIRST.SUBJECT THEN NUMBER = 0;
```

The same holds true for all the logical tests concerning the FIRST. and LAST. variables. In line ❷ you use the SUM statement (a statement in the form *variable + increment*) to increment the counter by one. Remember that the SUM statement causes the variable to be retained. Now, you may remember that the SUM statement also initializes variables to 0. Why do you need line ❶? Because you need to reset the counter to zero each time you reach a new subject. The output is shown next:

```
Counting Observations per Subject

Obs     SUBJECT     NUMBER

 1         1           3
 2         2           2
 3         3           1
 4         4           3
```

If you want to add the number of observations (NUMBER) to each observation in the original data set, you can do so with just a few lines of SAS code.

Program 3-5: Combining the Number of Observations with the Original Data

```
DATA COMBINE;
   MERGE ONE COUNT;
   BY SUBJECT;
RUN;

PROC PRINT DATA=COMBINE;
   TITLE "Listing of Data Set COMBINE";
RUN;
```

Here is the PROC PRINT listing:

```
Listing of Data Set COMBINE

Obs     SUBJECT     SCORE     NUMBER

 1         1          13         3
 2         1          12         3
 3         1          13         3
 4         2          22         2
 5         2          22         2
 6         3          31         1
 7         4          43         3
 8         4          42         3
 9         4          43         3
```

As you can see by inspecting the listing above, the new data set contains variables from the original data set plus the additional variable NUMBER, which represents the number of scores for each subject.

Knowing when you are processing the first or last observation for a subject or some other grouping variable is greatly simplified by creating FIRST. and LAST. temporary variables. You will see this powerful tool used frequently in the case studies in Chapters 9–11.

Flags and Counters

Introduction

This is a fairly strange chapter name. Sure, you know what counters are, but what do flags have to do with SAS programming? The term "flag" is an old programming term for a variable that keeps track of things. For example, if a patient comes into the clinic on several occasions and you want to keep track if he or she ever had a particular medical problem, you could assign a flag to that task. You could turn it on (typically by setting it equal to 1) if the problem ever occurred and leave it off (typically by setting it equal to 0) if the problem never occurred. Counters are similar in that they not only can keep track of events, but they can count the number of times the events have taken place. Retained variables and SUM statements will come in handy for these tasks.

Using a Flag Variable to Determine If a Particular Event Ever Occurred in Any One of Several Observations for Each Subject

To demonstrate the first flag variable example, you need to run Program 4-1 to create a simple patient visit data set.

Program 4-1: Creating a Test Data Set to Demonstrate Flags and Counters

```
DATA LAB;
   INPUT PATNO VISIT_NO OUTCOME;
DATALINES;
3 1 0
3 2 0
3 3 1
```

```
1 1 0
1 2 1
1 3 0
1 4 1
2 1 0
2 2 0
4 1 1
4 2 1
4 3 1
;
```

This data set consists of patient numbers (PATNO), visit number (VISIT_NO), and an outcome variable (OUTCOME). The first task is to create a new data set with one observation per patient, indicating if that patient *ever* had a positive outcome (equal to 1) for any visit. You want to "remember" the value of a variable from one observation to the next. The RETAIN lightbulb should be going off about now. By using a retained variable, you can "turn it on" if the outcome for any given patient is equal to 1. Since this variable is retained, the value will remain a 1 unless it is changed. Program 4-2 demonstrates how this works.

Program 4-2: Using a Flag Variable to "Remember" a Value from Previous Observations

```
PROC SORT DATA=LAB;   ❶
    BY PATNO VISIT_NO;
RUN;

DATA FLAG_TEST;
    SET LAB;
    BY PATNO;   ❷

    RETAIN FLAG; ***If FLAG = 1 outcome was positive;   ❸

    ***Initialize FLAG;
    IF FIRST.PATNO = 1 THEN FLAG = 0;   ❹

    ***Turn FLAG on if outcome is positive;
    IF OUTCOME = 1 THEN FLAG = 1;   ❺

    ***Output one observation when processing the last visit
        for a patient;
    IF LAST.PATNO = 1 THEN OUTPUT;   ❻
    DROP OUTCOME VISIT_NO;
RUN;
```

```
PROC PRINT DATA=FLAG_TEST;
   TITLE "Listing of Data Set FLAG_TEST";
RUN;
```

You first sort the original data set by PATNO and VISIT_NO so you can use the FIRST.PATNO and LAST.PATNO variables in the next DATA step. (Sorting by VISIT_NO is not necessary, but if you think you may need the data set in PATIENT-VISIT_NO order later on, you should do the sorting now.)

The BY statement in line ❷ creates the two temporary variables FIRST.PATNO and LAST.PATNO. In this program, the flag variable is called FLAG and it is retained (line ❸). (By the way, you can call this variable anything you want, we just chose the name FLAG in this example.) Next, you initialize the flag (set it equal to 0) for the first visit for each patient (line ❹). If the value of OUTCOME is 1 (true), you turn the flag on (set it equal to 1) ❺. In line ❻ you output a single observation for each patient. If the FLAG variable was ever set equal to 1, it will still be equal to 1 when this output occurs. It doesn't matter if OUTCOME was equal to 1 more than once—it will still remain a 1. The PROC PRINT listing is shown below:

```
Listing of Data Set FLAG_TEST

Obs      PATNO      FLAG

 1         1         1
 2         2         0
 3         3         1
 4         4         1
```

Counting the Number of Positive Outcomes for Each Patient

Not only can you keep track of patients with any positive outcomes, you can count the number of positive outcomes for each patient as well.

Program 4-3 uses a SUM statement to accomplish this. Remember that because you are using a SUM statement, you no longer need to explicitly retain the counting variable (but you must remember to reset it to 0 for each patient).

Program 4-3: Using a SUM Statement to Count the Number of Positive OUTCOMES for Each Patient

```
***Note: Data set lab already sorted;
DATA COUNT_TEST;
   SET LAB;
   BY PATNO;

   ***No need to RETAIN COUNT since it is used in a SUM statement
      and is therefore retained automatically;

   ***Initialize COUNT;
   IF FIRST.PATNO = 1 THEN COUNT = 0;    ❶

   ***Increment COUNT if outcome is positive;
   IF OUTCOME = 1 THEN COUNT + 1;    ❷

   ***Output one observation when processing the last visit
      for a patient;
   IF LAST.PATNO = 1 THEN OUTPUT;
   DROP OUTCOME;
RUN;
PROC PRINT DATA=COUNT_TEST;
   TITLE "Listing of Data Set COUNT_TEST";
RUN;
```

This program is perhaps even simpler than the previous program. Line ❶ initializes the counter to 0 for each patient and line ❷ adds one to the counter variable for each positive OUTCOME. You can even use the variable COUNT as an indicator if OUTCOME was ever equal to 1 (COUNT would be greater than 0). The PROC PRINT output is shown next:

```
Listing of Data Set COUNT_TEST

Obs     PATNO    VISIT_NO    COUNT

 1        1         4          2
 2        2         2          0
 3        3         3          1
 4        4         3          3
```

As you can see, a "flag" variable is a special case of a retained variable that takes on only two values: 1 or 0. Counters are also retained variables (either retained explicitly with a RETAIN statement or implicitly by using a SUM statement) that will count the number of events for each subject or group in your data set. You will see many applications using flags and counters in the case studies in Chapters 9–11.

Summarizing Data Using **PROC MEANS** and **PROC FREQ**

Introduction

Suppose you have a SAS data set containing student scores on a test. In this same data set, you also have the teacher's name, the name of the school, and the county. You may want to know the mean or other statistics for all the students; for all the students for a given teacher; for each teacher; for each school; or for each county. In addition, you may want these means in a SAS data set so you can perform further processing of the data. This chapter shows you how to use PROC MEANS and PROC FREQ to create a SAS data set of summary information.

Using PROC MEANS to Output Means to a Data Set

This first example uses a small data set consisting of student test scores, the teacher's name, the school, and the county. Run the Program Appendix-1 to create the sample data set. A complete listing of this data set is shown below:

```
Listing of Data Set TEST SCORES

Obs   COUNTY      SCHOOL                  TEACHER    MATH   SCIENCE   ENGLISH

  1   HUNTERDON   FLEMING MIDDLE SCHOOL   SMITH       92      95        88
  2   HUNTERDON   FLEMING MIDDLE SCHOOL   SMITH       94      89        92
  3   HUNTERDON   FLEMING MIDDLE SCHOOL   SMITH        .      82        84
  4   HUNTERDON   FLEMING MIDDLE SCHOOL   SMITH        .       .        68
  5   HUNTERDON   FLEMING MIDDLE SCHOOL   RIVERA      82      89        72
  6   HUNTERDON   FLEMING MIDDLE SCHOOL   RIVERA      97      94        92
  7   HUNTERDON   FLEMING MIDDLE SCHOOL   RIVERA       .      88         .
  8   HUNTERDON   ROBERT HUNTER           GREGORY     80      82        94
  9   HUNTERDON   ROBERT HUNTER           GREGORY     82      84        82
 10   HUNTERDON   ROBERT HUNTER           WRIGHT      60      70        80
 11   HUNTERDON   ROBERT HUNTER           WRIGHT      62      72        83
 12   MIDDLESEX   SAINT BARTS ACADEMY     JONES       72      78        77
 13   MIDDLESEX   SAINT BARTS ACADEMY     JONES       83      83        92
 14   MIDDLESEX   SAINT BARTS ACADEMY     JONES       91      78        81
 15   MIDDLESEX   RUTGERS PREP            MAROTTO      .      99         .
 16   MIDDLESEX   RUTGERS PREP            MAROTTO     96      98        98
 17   MIDDLESEX   RUTGERS PREP            MAROTTO     83      88        88
 18   MIDDLESEX   RUTGERS PREP            MAROTTO     84      86        85
 19   MIDDLESEX   RUTGERS PREP            MAROTTO     92      97        93
 20   MIDDLESEX   RUTGERS PREP            FRIEDMAN    99      98        90
 21   MIDDLESEX   RUTGERS PREP            FRIEDMAN    96      95        90
 22   MIDDLESEX   RUTGERS PREP            FRIEDMAN    84      85        84
 23   MIDDLESEX   RUTGERS PREP            PATERSON    68      72        66
 24   MIDDLESEX   RUTGERS PREP            PATERSON    72      74        68
 25   MIDDLESEX   FRANKLIN HIGH           PETERS      80      80        92
 26   MIDDLESEX   FRANKLIN HIGH           PETERS      83      85        88
```

As you can see, these teachers are very fortunate to have such small classes. Suppose you want to compute the mean math, science, and English test score for each teacher in the data set and you want these results in a SAS data set. Program 5-1 creates a new data set (TEACHER_MEANS) that does just that.

Program 5-1: Using a BY Statement in PROC MEANS to Create Means for Each TEACHER

```
PROC SORT DATA=TEST_SCORES;    ❶
   BY TEACHER;
RUN;

PROC MEANS DATA=TEST_SCORES NOPRINT;    ❷
   BY TEACHER;    ❸
   VAR MATH SCIENCE ENGLISH;
   OUTPUT OUT=TEACHER_MEANS    ❹
          MEAN=M_MATH M_SCIENCE M_ENGLISH;
RUN;
```

- Since you are using a BY statement with PROC MEANS, you must first sort the data set by the BY variable (TEACHER) ❶ (or be sure the data set was previously sorted).

- Next, the NOPRINT option is requested ❷ so that there will be no printed output—all that you want here is to create a SAS data set containing the teacher means. By the way, another procedure, PROC SUMMARY, is identical to PROC MEANS except that the default option is NOPRINT instead of PRINT. So you can substitute PROC SUMMARY for all the PROC MEANS examples and save a few keystrokes by not having to include the NOPRINT option.

- The BY statement ❸ instructs the procedure to compute statistics for each level of the BY variable; in this case, for each TEACHER.

- The OUTPUT statement ❹ is the key to having PROC MEANS create a SAS data set. The name following the OUT= option is the name of the SAS data set to be created. The list of variable names following the keyword MEAN= contains the three variable names that represent the means of the three variables listed in the VAR statement. In this example, the order of the variables in the list following the MEAN= option is in the same order as the variables listed in the VAR statement. The three variables following the MEAN= option could have been called MANNY, MOE, and JACK. MANNY would have represented the mean MATH score, MOE, the mean SCIENCE score, and JACK, the mean ENGLISH score.

Running PROC PRINT on this data set produces the following listing:

```
Listing of Data Set TEACHER_MEANS

Obs     TEACHER     _TYPE_     _FREQ_     M_MATH     M_SCIENCE     M_ENGLISH
 1      FRIEDMAN       0          3        93.00      92.6667       88.0000
 2      GREGORY        0          2        81.00      83.0000       88.0000
 3      JONES          0          3        82.00      79.6667       83.3333
 4      MAROTTO        0          5        88.75      93.6000       91.0000
 5      PATERSON       0          2        70.00      73.0000       67.0000
 6      PETERS         0          2        81.50      82.5000       90.0000
 7      RIVERA         0          3        89.50      90.3333       82.0000
 8      SMITH          0          4        93.00      88.6667       83.0000
 9      WRIGHT         0          2        61.00      71.0000       81.5000
```

Notice that there is one observation per teacher. The two variables _TYPE_ and _FREQ_ were added to the data set by PROC MEANS. In this example, the _TYPE_ variable is of no interest to us (we'll discuss this variable later when we use a CLASS statement instead of a BY statement). The variable _FREQ_ tells you the number of observations in each level of the BY variable. In this example, _FREQ_ represents the number of students for each of the teachers.

Another way to create this same data set (well, almost the same) is to use a CLASS statement instead of a BY statement. Program 5-2 is identical to Program 5-1 except that a CLASS statement is used instead of a BY statement. Since a CLASS statement does not require the data set to be sorted, the sort procedure is omitted as well.

Program 5-2: Using a CLASS Statement in PROC MEANS to Create Means for Each TEACHER

```
PROC MEANS DATA=TEST_SCORES NOPRINT;
    CLASS TEACHER;   ❶
    VAR MATH SCIENCE ENGLISH;
    OUTPUT OUT=TEACHER_MEANS
           MEAN=M_MATH M_SCIENCE M_ENGLISH;
RUN;
```

A listing of this data set is shown next:

```
Listing of Data Set TEACHER_MEANS

Obs     TEACHER     _TYPE_     _FREQ_      M_MATH      M_SCIENCE      M_ENGLISH

 1                     0         26       83.2727      85.6400        84.4583
 2     FRIEDMAN        1          3       93.0000      92.6667        88.0000
 3     GREGORY         1          2       81.0000      83.0000        88.0000
 4     JONES           1          3       82.0000      79.6667        83.3333
 5     MAROTTO         1          5       88.7500      93.6000        91.0000
 6     PATERSON        1          2       70.0000      73.0000        67.0000
 7     PETERS          1          2       81.5000      82.5000        90.0000
 8     RIVERA          1          3       89.5000      90.3333        82.0000
 9     SMITH           1          4       93.0000      88.6667        83.0000
10     WRIGHT          1          2       61.0000      71.0000        81.5000
```

This data set looks very much like the previous one except that there is one extra observation and the values of _TYPE_ are different. Herein lies one of the differences between using a BY statement and a CLASS statement. In this example, the first observation (_TYPE_ = 0) represents the mean of all the students (called a "grand mean" by statisticians, called "the whole enchilada" by nonstatisticians). If you only want the means for each TEACHER, you can include the NWAY procedure option like this:

```
PROC MEANS DATA=TEST_SCORES NWAY NOPRINT;
```

If you run Program 5-2 with the NWAY option added, the resulting data set will be identical to the listing above except that the first observation (_TYPE_ = 0) will be omitted.

Comparing CLASS and BY Statements with PROC MEANS

Notice that in the first two programs in this chapter, one used a BY statement (Program 5-1) and one used a CLASS statement (Program 5-2). What are the advantages and disadvantages of each? First, if all you want is summary statistics broken down by each of the BY or CLASS variables, you may want to use a BY statement if the data set has already been sorted by these variables for some other purpose. If the data set is large and you have no other reason to sort it, you may be better off using a CLASS statement. If you have a large number of CLASS variables and if some of the CLASS variables have many possible values (such as a subject number), you may run into memory problems on some computing platforms and be forced to sort and use a BY statement. If this is the case, you should see an error message in the SAS log telling you about the memory problem. Using a BY statement results in an output data set that is similar to one you would obtain by using a CLASS statement and the NWAY option. That is, when you use a BY statement, you only get the cell means. If you want to use a TYPES statement (described later in this chapter) to select specific combinations of class variables, you must use a CLASS statement—a BY statement does not allow you to use this option. Finally, note that CLASS statements are only available with certain procedures while BY statements are more general and can be used with most procedures that produce statistical output such as PROC FREQ (which does not allow a CLASS statement).

Computing Other Descriptive Statistics

You can have PROC MEANS output many other descriptive statistics. You need to list the keywords in the OUTPUT statement and provide variable names to represent each of these values. For example, suppose in addition to the mean test scores for each teacher, you want to know the median, the mean, and the number of nonmissing values used to compute each mean. Program 5-3 will do just that.

Program 5-3: Using PROC MEANS to Output Other Descriptive Statistics

```
PROC MEANS DATA=TEST_SCORES NOPRINT NWAY;
   CLASS TEACHER;
   VAR MATH SCIENCE ENGLISH;
   OUTPUT OUT = TEACHER_MEANS (DROP = _TYPE_)
         MEAN = M_MATH M_SCIENCE M_ENGLISH
         MEDIAN = MED_MATH MED_SCIENCE MED_ENGLISH
         N = N_MATH N_SCIENCE N_ENGLISH;
RUN;
```

The data set option DROP= was added to eliminate the _TYPE_ variable from the resulting data set. Since it's the same value for every observation, you don't really need it. The keywords MEAN=, MEDIAN=, and N= are used to output each of these descriptive statistics. Other useful output keywords are

Keyword	Description
NMISS	Number of missing values
MIN	Smallest nonmissing value
MAX	Largest value
RANGE	Range - difference between the minimum and maximum values
Q1	25th percentile
Q3	75th percentile
QRANGE	Interquartile range (difference between 25th and 75th percentile)
STD	Standard deviation
STDERR	Standard error

A complete list of output statistics can be found in the *SAS Procedures Guide, Version 8, Volumes 1 and 2*, published by SAS (Pubcode 57238) and under the MEANS Procedure in SAS OnlineDoc. (Note that MEDIAN, Q1, Q3, and QRANGE are relatively recent additions to SAS.)

A listing of the TEACHER_MEANS data set created by running this program is shown next:

```
Listing of Data Set TEACHER_MEANS

Obs     TEACHER     _FREQ_    M_MATH    M_SCIENCE    M_ENGLISH    MED_MATH

 1      FRIEDMAN      3        93.00      92.6667      88.0000      96.0
 2      GREGORY       2        81.00      83.0000      88.0000      81.0
 3      JONES         3        82.00      79.6667      83.3333      83.0
 4      MAROTTO       5        88.75      93.6000      91.0000      88.0
 5      PATERSON      2        70.00      73.0000      67.0000      70.0
 6      PETERS        2        81.50      82.5000      90.0000      81.5
 7      RIVERA        3        89.50      90.3333      82.0000      89.5
 8      SMITH         4        93.00      88.6667      83.0000      93.0
 9      WRIGHT        2        61.00      71.0000      81.5000      61.0
```

Obs	MED_SCIENCE	MED_ENGLISH	N_MATH	N_SCIENCE	N_ENGLISH
1	95.0	90.0	3	3	3
2	83.0	88.0	2	2	2
3	78.0	81.0	3	3	3
4	97.0	90.5	4	5	4
5	73.0	67.0	2	2	2
6	82.5	90.0	2	2	2
7	89.0	82.0	2	3	2
8	89.0	86.0	2	3	4
9	71.0	81.5	2	2	2

Automatically Naming the Variables in the Output Data Set

A new output option called AUTONAME was added to SAS starting with Version 7. When you use this option, PROC MEANS adds the statistics keyword to the variable name to create new names for variables requested in the output data set. For example, Program 5-4 produces the same output as Program 5-3, except that the variable names for the requested statistics are now created automatically. Program 5-4 demonstrates the AUTONAME option.

Program 5-4: Demonstrating the AUTONAME Option of PROC MEANS

```
PROC MEANS DATA=TEST_SCORES NOPRINT NWAY;
   CLASS TEACHER;
   VAR MATH SCIENCE ENGLISH;
   OUTPUT OUT = TEACHER_MEANS (DROP = _TYPE_)
          MEAN =
          MEDIAN =
          N = / AUTONAME;
RUN;
```

Inspection of the listing below shows that the AUTONAME option works as designed:

```
Listing of Data Set TEACHER_MEANS

                       MATH_    SCIENCE_   ENGLISH_    MATH_
Obs    TEACHER    _FREQ_  Mean     Mean        Mean     Median

 1     FRIEDMAN      3   93.00   92.6667    88.0000    96.0
 2     GREGORY       2   81.00   83.0000    88.0000    81.0
 3     JONES         3   82.00   79.6667    83.3333    83.0
 4     MAROTTO       5   88.75   93.6000    91.0000    88.0
 5     PATERSON      2   70.00   73.0000    67.0000    70.0
 6     PETERS        2   81.50   82.5000    90.0000    81.5
 7     RIVERA        3   89.50   90.3333    82.0000    89.5
 8     SMITH         4   93.00   88.6667    83.0000    93.0
 9     WRIGHT        2   61.00   71.0000    81.5000    61.0

       SCIENCE_   ENGLISH_               SCIENCE_   ENGLISH_
Obs    Median     Median     MATH_N        N          N

 1      95.0       90.0        3           3          3
 2      83.0       88.0        2           2          2
 3      78.0       81.0        3           3          3
 4      97.0       90.5        4           5          4
 5      73.0       67.0        2           2          2
 6      82.5       90.0        2           2          2
 7      89.0       82.0        2           3          2
 8      89.0       86.0        2           3          4
 9      71.0       81.5        2           2          2
```

Demonstrating an Alternative Way to Select Specific Descriptive Statistics for Selected Variables

Suppose you want the mean test score, by teacher, for the science and English scores, the median score for math, and the number of nonmissing observations for all three scores. One way to accomplish this is to run Program 5-3 and use the DROP= data set option to delete the unwanted variables. An alternative approach is shown in Program 5-5. Following each of the keywords such as MEAN or MEDIAN, you provide a list of variables in parentheses. Then, following the equal sign, you provide a list of variable names for the requested statistic (in the same order as the variables listed in parentheses). You can omit the VAR statement when using this technique, as long as all the variables you want are listed somewhere in the lists following the keywords, although a VAR list may be useful for clarity.

Program 5-5: Demonstrating an Alternative Way of Specifying Descriptive Statistics

```
PROC MEANS DATA=TEST_SCORES NOPRINT NWAY;
   CLASS TEACHER;
   VAR MATH SCIENCE ENGLISH;
   OUTPUT OUT = TEACHER_MEANS(DROP = _TYPE_)
          MEAN(SCIENCE ENGLISH) = M_SCIENCE M_ENGLISH
          MEDIAN(MATH) = MED_MATH
          N = N_MATH N_SCIENCE N_ENGLISH;
RUN;
```

When you run Program 5-5, the resulting data set contains the specific descriptive statistics requested.

```
Listing of Data Set TEACHER_MEANS

Obs  TEACHER    _FREQ_  M_SCIENCE  M_ENGLISH  MED_MATH  N_MATH  N_SCIENCE  N_ENGLISH

 1   FRIEDMAN     3      92.6667    88.0000     96.0       3        3          3
 2   GREGORY      2      83.0000    88.0000     81.0       2        2          2
 3   JONES        3      79.6667    83.3333     83.0       3        3          3
 4   MAROTTO      5      93.6000    91.0000     88.0       4        5          4
 5   PATERSON     2      73.0000    67.0000     70.0       2        2          2
 6   PETERS       2      82.5000    90.0000     81.5       2        2          2
 7   RIVERA       3      90.3333    82.0000     89.5       2        3          2
 8   SMITH        4      88.6667    83.0000     93.0       2        3          4
 9   WRIGHT       2      71.0000    81.5000     61.0       2        2          2
```

Adding Additional Variables to the Summary Data Set Using an ID Statement

Suppose you want to see summary statistics broken down by TEACHER and you want the resulting summary data set to include the name of the school along with the other summary variables. This is where an ID statement comes in handy. Normally, the output data set contains all the variables listed in the CLASS statement and all the summary statistics variables listed after the keywords (such as MEAN= or N=). You may include a list of variables in an ID statement if you want them included in the output data set. (A note of caution here: The ID variable must be more "general" than the CLASS variable. For example, if you have SCHOOL as the CLASS variable and TEACHER as the ID variable, you will get incorrect results—a single value of TEACHER (by default, the maximum) for each SCHOOL.) Program 5-6 uses an ID statement to include the school names in the output data set.

Program 5-6: Using an ID Statement to Include Additional Variables in the Output Data Set

```
PROC MEANS DATA=TEST_SCORES NOPRINT NWAY;
   CLASS TEACHER;
   ID SCHOOL;
   VAR MATH SCIENCE ENGLISH;
   OUTPUT OUT=TEACHER_MEANS(DROP=_TYPE_)
          MEAN=M_MATH M_SCIENCE M_ENGLISH;
RUN;
```

A listing of the output data set is shown next:

```
Listing of Data Set TEACHER_MEANS

Obs   TEACHER    SCHOOL                 _FREQ_   M_MATH   M_SCIENCE   M_ENGLISH

 1    FRIEDMAN   RUTGERS PREP              3      93.00    92.6667     88.0000
 2    GREGORY    ROBERT HUNTER             2      81.00    83.0000     88.0000
 3    JONES      SAINT BARTS ACADEMY       3      82.00    79.6667     83.3333
 4    MAROTTO    RUTGERS PREP              5      88.75    93.6000     91.0000
 5    PATERSON   RUTGERS PREP              2      70.00    73.0000     67.0000
 6    PETERS     FRANKLIN HIGH             2      81.50    82.5000     90.0000
 7    RIVERA     FLEMING MIDDLE SCHOOL     3      89.50    90.3333     82.0000
 8    SMITH      FLEMING MIDDLE SCHOOL     4      93.00    88.6667     83.0000
 9    WRIGHT     ROBERT HUNTER             2      61.00    71.0000     81.5000
```

Specifying More Than One CLASS Variable

Here is where things get complicated. Let's first add one additional variable (school size) to the TEST_SCORES data set. Program 5-7 creates a small data set with the school size information and merges it with the TEST_SCORES data set to create a new data set.

Program 5-7: Creating a New Data Set Including the School Size

```
DATA SCHOOL_SIZE;
   INPUT @1  SCHOOL  $21.
         @23 SIZE    $5.;
DATALINES;
FLEMING MIDDLE SCHOOL SMALL
ROBERT HUNTER         LARGE
SAINT BARTS ACADEMY   SMALL
RUTGERS PREP          SMALL
FRANKLIN HIGH         LARGE
;
PROC SORT DATA=TEST_SCORES;
   BY SCHOOL;
RUN;
PROC SORT DATA=SCHOOL_SIZE;
   BY SCHOOL;
RUN;
DATA COMBINED;
   MERGE TEST_SCORES SCHOOL_SIZE;
   BY SCHOOL;
RUN;
PROC PRINT DATA=COMBINED;
   TITLE "Listing of Data Set COMBINED";
RUN;
```

The new combined data set is listed next.

```
Listing of Data Set COMBINED

Obs   COUNTY     SCHOOL                      TEACHER   MATH SCIENCE ENGLISH SIZE

  1  HUNTERDON  FLEMING  MIDDLE  SCHOOL  RIVERA      82      89      72   SMALL
  2  HUNTERDON  FLEMING  MIDDLE  SCHOOL  RIVERA      97      94      92   SMALL
  3  HUNTERDON  FLEMING  MIDDLE  SCHOOL  RIVERA       .      88       .   SMALL
  4  HUNTERDON  FLEMING  MIDDLE  SCHOOL  SMITH       92      95      88   SMALL
  5  HUNTERDON  FLEMING  MIDDLE  SCHOOL  SMITH       94      89      92   SMALL
  6  HUNTERDON  FLEMING  MIDDLE  SCHOOL  SMITH        .      82      84   SMALL
  7  HUNTERDON  FLEMING  MIDDLE  SCHOOL  SMITH        .       .      68   SMALL
  8  MIDDLESEX  FRANKLIN HIGH            PETERS      80      80      92   LARGE
  9  MIDDLESEX  FRANKLIN HIGH            PETERS      83      85      88   LARGE
 10  HUNTERDON  ROBERT  HUNTER           GREGORY     80      82      94   LARGE
 11  HUNTERDON  ROBERT  HUNTER           GREGORY     82      84      82   LARGE
 12  HUNTERDON  ROBERT  HUNTER           WRIGHT      60      70      80   LARGE
 13  HUNTERDON  ROBERT  HUNTER           WRIGHT      62      72      83   LARGE
 14  MIDDLESEX  RUTGERS PREP             FRIEDMAN    99      98      90   SMALL
 15  MIDDLESEX  RUTGERS PREP             FRIEDMAN    96      95      90   SMALL
 16  MIDDLESEX  RUTGERS PREP             FRIEDMAN    84      85      84   SMALL
 17  MIDDLESEX  RUTGERS PREP             MAROTTO      .      99       .   SMALL
 18  MIDDLESEX  RUTGERS PREP             MAROTTO     96      98      98   SMALL
 19  MIDDLESEX  RUTGERS PREP             MAROTTO     83      88      88   SMALL
 20  MIDDLESEX  RUTGERS PREP             MAROTTO     84      86      85   SMALL
 21  MIDDLESEX  RUTGERS PREP             MAROTTO     92      97      93   SMALL
 22  MIDDLESEX  RUTGERS PREP             PATERSON    68      72      66   SMALL
 23  MIDDLESEX  RUTGERS PREP             PATERSON    72      74      68   SMALL
 24  MIDDLESEX  SAINT  BARTS  ACADEMY    JONES       72      78      77   SMALL
 25  MIDDLESEX  SAINT  BARTS  ACADEMY    JONES       83      83      92   SMALL
 26  MIDDLESEX  SAINT  BARTS  ACADEMY    JONES       91      78      81   SMALL
```

Now you are ready to see what happens when you use more than one CLASS variable. Let's look at mean test scores, broken down by COUNTY and SIZE.

Program 5-8: Demonstrating More Than One CLASS Variable

```
PROC MEANS DATA=COMBINED NOPRINT;
   CLASS COUNTY SIZE;
   VAR MATH SCIENCE ENGLISH;
   OUTPUT OUT = COUNTY_BY_SIZE
          MEAN = M_MATH M_SCIENCE M_ENGLISH;
RUN;
PROC PRINT DATA=COUNTY_BY_SIZE;
   TITLE "Listing of Data Set COUNTY_BY_SIZE";
RUN;
```

```
Listing of Data Set COUNTY_BY_SIZE

Obs    COUNTY      SIZE     _TYPE_    _FREQ_     M_MATH     M_SCIENCE    M_ENGLISH

 1                             0        26       83.2727     85.6400      84.4583
 2                  LARGE      1         6       74.5000     78.8333      86.5000
 3                  SMALL      1        20       86.5625     87.7895      83.7778
 4     HUNTERDON              2        11       81.1250     84.5000      83.5000
 5     MIDDLESEX             2        15       84.5000     86.4000      85.1429
 6     HUNTERDON   LARGE      3         4       71.0000     77.0000      84.7500
 7     HUNTERDON   SMALL      3         7       91.2500     89.5000      82.6667
 8     MIDDLESEX   LARGE      3         2       81.5000     82.5000      90.0000
 9     MIDDLESEX   SMALL      3        13       85.0000     87.0000      84.3333
```

Notice that the values of _TYPE_ now range from 0 to 3. It is clear from inspection of the listing, that the _TYPE_ = 0 observation is the mean of all 26 observations (the grand mean). The next two observations (_TYPE_ = 1) represent the mean scores broken down by school size. You can tell this because there are missing values for COUNTY and the values of "LARGE" and "SMALL" for SIZE. The two observations with _TYPE_ = 1 represent the means of the test scores for each of the two school sizes. The _TYPE_ = 2 observations that come next represent the means broken down by COUNTY. Finally, the _TYPE_ = 3 observations represent the means broken down by COUNTY and SIZE.

There is a relationship between the value of the _TYPE_ variable and what the means (or other statistics) represent. It is a bit complicated, so bear with me. (Beginning with Version 7, there are other tools to help with this process. They will be discussed later in this chapter.) Look at the following diagram:

CLASS Variables		Representation	
COUNTY	SIZE	Binary	Decimal
0	0	00	0
0	1	01	1
1	0	10	2
1	1	11	3

The left two columns represent the two CLASS variables in the order they appear in the CLASS statement. Under each of these variables, you start counting in binary: 00, 01, 10, 11. The decimal equivalents of the binary representations are shown in the last column.

Now for the rule: Any time a 1 appears under the variable, the means (or other statistics) are broken down by that variable. For example, the row of the table with a binary 10 (decimal value of 2) represents mean scores broken down by COUNTY (regardless of SIZE). Thus, the _TYPE_ = 2 observations represent COUNTY means.

Since this is so complicated, some new features were added to PROC MEANS to help select which combinations of CLASS variables you want in the output data set.

Selecting Multi-Way Breakdowns Using the TYPES Statement

Suppose you want to see mean test scores both by SIZE and for each combination of COUNTY and SIZE (but not the grand mean or by COUNTY). You could just run Program 5-8 and follow it with a DATA step with a subsetting IF (or WHERE) statement. Program 5-9 demonstrates such a DATA step.

Program 5-9: Selecting Only Certain Breakdowns of CLASS Variables

```
DATA SELECT;
   SET COUNTY_BY_SIZE;
   WHERE _TYPE_ IN (1 3);
RUN;
```

The data set SELECT now contains only means by SIZE and means for each combination of COUNTY and SIZE. You can save time and effort by using a TYPES statement to request exactly which breakdowns you want, directly in PROC MEANS. The TYPES statement allows you to specify breakdowns by listing the CLASS variables and the interactions you want. For example, if you have four CLASS variables (A, B, C, and D), you might write statements such as these:

```
TYPES A A*C D*C;   ❶
TYPES A*(B C D);   ❷
TYPES () A A*C*D;  ❸
```

Line ❶ requests means for each level of A and for the two-way breakdowns A by C and D by C. Line ❷ is a shortcut way of requesting breakdowns A*B, A*C, and A*D. Finally, line ❸ requests the grand mean (represented by the set of parentheses), means for each level of A, and for the three-way breakdown A*C*D.

Getting back to our sample data set, to output means broken down by SIZE and COUNTY by SIZE, you could run Program 5-10.

Program 5-10: Using a TYPES Statement to Specify Breakdowns

```
PROC MEANS DATA=COMBINED NOPRINT;
   CLASS COUNTY SIZE;
   TYPES SIZE COUNTY*SIZE;   ❶
   VAR MATH SCIENCE ENGLISH;
   OUTPUT OUT = COUNTY_SIZE
         MEAN = M_MATH M_SCIENCE M_ENGLISH;
RUN;
```

Line ❶ requests that only breakdowns by SIZE and COUNTY by SIZE are required. The listing of the output data set follows:

```
Listing of Data Set COUNTY_SIZE with the TYPES Option

Obs   COUNTY     SIZE   _TYPE_   _FREQ_   M_MATH   M_SCIENCE   M_ENGLISH

 1               LARGE    1         6     74.5000    78.8333    86.5000
 2               SMALL    1        20     86.5625    87.7895    83.7778
 3    HUNTERDON  LARGE    3         4     71.0000    77.0000    84.7500
 4    HUNTERDON  SMALL    3         7     91.2500    89.5000    82.6667
 5    MIDDLESEX  LARGE    3         2     81.5000    82.5000    90.0000
 6    MIDDLESEX  SMALL    3        13     85.0000    87.0000    84.3333
```

Notice that the data set only contains the requested breakdowns. If you want each of the _TYPE_ observations in a separate data set, you could use multiple OUTPUT statements in a single PROC MEANS (each data set name is followed by a WHERE= data set option specifying which _TYPE_ value you want), or you could follow Program 5-10 with a short DATA step as demonstrated in Program 5-11.

Program 5-11: Separating the _TYPE_ Observations into Separate Data Sets

```
DATA SIZE COUNTY_BY_SIZE;
   SET COUNTY_SIZE;
   IF _TYPE_ = 1 THEN OUTPUT SIZE;    ❶
   ELSE IF _TYPE_ = 3 THEN OUTPUT COUNTY_BY_SIZE;    ❷
RUN;
```

An alternative to lines ❶ and ❷ in Program 5-11 is to represent the value of the _TYPE_ variable in binary. These two lines could be replaced by the two statements below:

```
IF _TYPE_ = '01'B THEN OUTPUT SIZE;
ELSE IF _TYPE_ = '11'B THEN OUTPUT COUNTY_BY_SIZE;
```

The 0's and 1's in quotes followed by the letter "B" represent binary literals. You may already be familiar with date or hex literals. The form of a binary literal is the binary string in single or double quotes, followed by a lowercase or uppercase "B."

Just when you learned a new trick, you no longer need it! Beginning with Version 7, SAS includes the CHARTYPE option for PROC MEANS. The next section describes how this works.

Using the PROC MEANS CHARTYPE Option to Simplify the _TYPE_ Interpretation

By including the procedure option CHARTYPE with PROC MEANS, the _TYPE_ variable is turned into a character variable representing the binary string previously described. Thus, if you included the CHARTYPE option in Program 5-10, this program and the short DATA step that followed (Program 5-11) could be replaced by Program 5-12.

Program 5-12: Demonstrating the CHARTYPE Option of PROC MEANS

```
PROC MEANS DATA=COMBINED NOPRINT CHARTYPE;
   CLASS COUNTY SIZE;
   TYPES SIZE COUNTY*SIZE;    ❶
   VAR MATH SCIENCE ENGLISH;
   OUTPUT OUT = COUNTY_SIZE
        MEAN = M_MATH M_SCIENCE M_ENGLISH;
RUN;
```

```
DATA SIZE COUNTY_BY_SIZE;
   SET COUNTY_SIZE;
   IF _TYPE_ = '01' THEN OUTPUT SIZE;   ❶
   ELSE IF _TYPE_ = '11' THEN OUTPUT COUNTY_BY_SIZE;   ❷
RUN;
```

Notice that the character strings (lines ❶ and ❷) are not binary literals—they are simply character values.

Comparing PROC MEANS and PROC FREQ for Creating an Output Data Set Containing Counts

You already saw that you can use PROC MEANS to count the number of observations in a subgroup, such as the number of students for each teacher. Remember that the variable _FREQ_ represents the number of observations making up the subgroup while the statistic N= represents the number of nonmissing values for a variable in that subgroup.

Suppose you want to know how many students are assigned to each teacher in the TEST_SCORES data set. One way is to use PROC MEANS on *any numeric variable* in the data set, broken down by TEACHER as shown in Program 5-13.

Program 5-13: Using PROC MEANS to Create an Output Data Set Containing Counts

```
PROC MEANS DATA=TEST_SCORES NOPRINT NWAY;
   CLASS TEACHER;
   VAR MATH;
   OUTPUT OUT = STUDENT_COUNT(DROP=DUMMY _TYPE_
                       RENAME=(_FREQ_ = N_STUDENTS))
          MEAN = DUMMY;
RUN;

PROC PRINT DATA=STUDENT_COUNT;
   TITLE "Listing of Data Set STUDENT_COUNT";
RUN;
```

The resulting listing contains only the teacher name (the CLASS variable) plus a variable called N_STUDENTS (renamed from _FREQ_), which represents the number of students for each teacher.

```
Listing of Data Set STUDENT_COUNT

Obs      TEACHER      N_STUDENTS

 1       FRIEDMAN         3
 2       GREGORY          2
 3       JONES            3
 4       MAROTTO          5
 5       PATERSON         2
 6       PETERS           2
 7       RIVERA           3
 8       SMITH            4
 9       WRIGHT           2
```

By the way, you can omit the VAR statement entirely, but if you do so, the resulting data set will contain much more information than you will ever need or want. It is definitely better to include a numeric variable in a VAR statement as shown here.

You can accomplish exactly the same goal by using PROC FREQ instead of PROC MEANS to create the data set, as demonstrated in Program 5-14. This is particularly useful when there are no numeric variables in the data set.

Program 5-14: Using PROC FREQ to Create an Output Data Set Containing Counts

```
PROC FREQ DATA=TEST_SCORES NOPRINT;
   TABLES TEACHER / OUT = STUDENT_COUNT(DROP = PERCENT
                                        RENAME=(COUNT = N_STUDENTS));
RUN;

PROC PRINT DATA=STUDENT_COUNT;
   TITLE "Listing of Data Set STUDENT_COUNT";
RUN;
```

The data set created by the OUT= TABLES option of PROC FREQ contains all the variables in the TABLES statement plus two additional variables, COUNT and PERCENT. The values of COUNT represent the frequencies for the variables listed in the TABLES statement (similar to the variable called _FREQ_ produced by PROC MEANS). The variable PERCENT is the same as the values of percent that you see on the printed output from PROC FREQ. In this example, a RENAME= data set option was used to rename COUNT to N_STUDENTS and a DROP= data set option was used to eliminate the PERCENT variable from the output data set. There is no need to show you the listing of the data set STUDENT_COUNT since it is identical to the listing above produced by PROC MEANS.

Counting Frequencies for a Two-Way Table

The technique of using an OUT= TABLES option with PROC FREQ also works with two-way tables. If you want the number of large and small schools in each of the counties, you can run Program 5-15.

Program 5-15: Using PROC FREQ to Output Counts for a Two-Way Table

```
PROC FREQ DATA=COMBINED NOPRINT;
   TABLES COUNTY*SIZE / OUT = COUNTY_SIZE(DROP = PERCENT);
RUN;

PROC PRINT DATA=COUNTY_SIZE;
   TITLE "Listing of Data Set COUNTY_SIZE";
RUN;
```

Note: In this example, the variable name COUNT was not renamed. A listing of the resulting data set is shown next:

```
Listing of Data Set COUNTY_SIZE

Obs       COUNTY       SIZE      COUNT

 1        HUNTERDON    LARGE        4
 2        HUNTERDON    SMALL        7
 3        MIDDLESEX    LARGE        2
 4        MIDDLESEX    SMALL       13
```

If you include more than one TABLE request with a single TABLES statement, the output data set will only contain frequencies for the last requested table. If you want to produce several output data sets, you can use separate TABLES statements. For example, to obtain counts for both COUNTY and SIZE, you could write

```
PROC FREQ DATA=COMBINED NOPRINT;
   TABLES COUNTY / OUT = N_COUNTY(DROP = PERCENT);
   TABLES SIZE / OUT = N_SIZE(DROP = PERCENT);
RUN;
```

Creating summary data sets has many uses. Sometimes you want to produce means or counts on individuals. At other times, you want to summarize data based on one or more CLASS variables. Understanding the concepts in this chapter will place these powerful summarizing procedures in your bag of SAS tools. If you use PROC MEANS (or SUMMARY) beginning with Version 7, added features such as the TYPES statement and AUTONAME option in the OUTPUT statement and the CHARTYPE procedure option give you considerable control in how the statistics should be broken down and used in subsequent DATA steps.

Using PROC SQL with Longitudinal Data

Introduction

A SAS procedure called PROC SQL (which stands for Structured Query Language and is pronounced "sea quell" or spelled out as S-Q-L) provides you with an alternative or addition to DATA step programming. There are several applications of SQL to longitudinal data where one SQL query can replace several DATA steps. SQL is especially useful when you want to combine summary information (such as a count of the number of observations for each subject) with the original data set).

This chapter shows a few examples of how PROC SQL can be used to solve the same types of longitudinal data manipulations described in some of the earlier chapters. Readers are referred to several of the excellent books and manuals published by SAS for more complete information on PROC SQL.

Creating a Demonstration Data Set

First, we need a small data set to "play" with. Run Program 6-1 to create a data set called SQL_TEST.

Program 6-1: Creating the Data Set SQL_TEST

```
DATA SQL_TEST;
    INPUT SUBJECT $ DAY $ X Y Z;
DATALINES;
1 MONDAY 10 20 30
1 FRIDAY 11 21 31
2 THURSDAY 30 . 34
3 MONDAY 11 22 33
3 TUESDAY 13 14 15
3 FRIDAY 14 19 21
4 FRIDAY 40 50 60
4 SATURDAY 41 42 .
5 TUESDAY 5 6 7
5 FRIDAY 6 7 8
5 SUNDAY 8 9 10
7 MONDAY 10 13 14
7 THURSDAY 14 . 22
;
PROC PRINT DATA=SQL_TEST;
    TITLE "Listing of Data Set SQL_TEST";
    ID SUBJECT;
RUN;
```

A listing of this data set follows:

```
Listing of Data Set SQL_TEST

SUBJECT        DAY        X      Y      Z

   1         MONDAY      10     20     30
   1         FRIDAY      11     21     31
   2         THURSDAY    30      .     34
   3         MONDAY      11     22     33
   3         TUESDAY     13     14     15
   3         FRIDAY      14     19     21
   4         FRIDAY      40     50     60
   4         SATURDAY    41     42      .
   5         TUESDAY      5      6      7
   5         FRIDAY       6      7      8
   5         SUNDAY       8      9     10
   7         MONDAY      10     13     14
   7         THURSDAY    14      .     22
```

As you can see, each subject has from one to three observations.

A Simple SQL Query

Let's start out with a very basic SQL query. Program 6-2 selects the subject number (SUBJECT) and the variables X, Y, and Z from the SQL_TEST data set (or table as it is called in SQL terminology). Since there is no CREATE TABLE statement in this query, running the query will give you a listing of the results.

Program 6-2: Using PROC SQL to List the Observations from a SAS Data Set

```
PROC SQL;
    TITLE "Output from Program 6-2";
    SELECT SUBJECT, X, Y, Z   ❶
    FROM SQL_TEST;   ❷
QUIT;
```

The SELECT clause ❶ says to select the four variables listed. For those of you (like the author) who are used to traditional SAS DATA step syntax, you need to remember to separate the variable names in a SELECT statement with commas, not spaces. The FROM clause in this query tells the procedure which data set you want to query. Unlike other SAS procedures, the order of these statements is important: the SELECT statement must precede the FROM statement. You do not need a RUN statement—the query is performed as soon as the required statements are submitted. The QUIT statement is included since PROC SQL indicates that it is still running unless you submit a QUIT statement or run another procedure or a DATA step. The result is a simple listing of the data set as shown next:

SUBJECT	X	Y	Z
1	10	20	30
1	11	21	31
2	30	.	34
3	11	22	33
3	13	14	15
3	14	19	21
4	40	50	60
4	41	42	.
5	5	6	7
5	6	7	8
5	8	9	10
7	10	13	14
7	14	.	22

Using PROC SQL to Count Observations within a BY Group

You will find that the GROUP BY clause is very useful for performing longitudinal operations on your data. GROUP BY alone simply places observations with the same grouping variable together. Combining this clause with a COUNT function demonstrates one of the ways in which PROC SQL can be used with longitudinal data. Inspection of Program 6-3 shows how you can use these two features to your advantage.

Program 6-3: Adding a GROUP BY Clause and a COUNT Function to the SQL Query

```
PROC SQL;
   TITLE "Output from Program 6-3";
   SELECT SUBJECT, X, Y, Z,
          COUNT(SUBJECT) AS NUMBER   ❶
   FROM SQL_TEST
   GROUP BY SUBJECT;   ❷
QUIT;
```

The GROUP BY clause ❷ is needed so that the COUNT function operates on each value of SUBJECT as a group. Because of line ❷ the COUNT function ❶ counts the number of observations for each unique subject number. The SELECT statement also allows you to provide a variable name (called an alias) for this result by placing this variable name after the keyword AS. So when you inspect the listing below, you will see a column labeled NUMBER, which is the number of visits for each subject.

SUBJECT	X	Y	Z	NUMBER
1	10	20	30	2
1	11	21	31	2
2	30	.	34	1
3	14	19	21	3
3	13	14	15	3
3	11	22	33	3
4	40	50	60	2
4	41	42	.	2
5	8	9	10	3
5	6	7	8	3
5	5	6	7	3
7	14	.	22	2
7	10	13	14	2

Being able to count observations in a group can be used in several ways. First, by combining it with a HAVING clause, you can subset your data set, selecting all subjects with a specified number of visits. Let's demonstrate this before we go on to other applications.

Demonstrating a HAVING Clause

Program 6-4 demonstrates the use of a HAVING clause to subset the resulting data set.

Program 6-4: Adding a HAVING Clause to Subset a Data Set

```
PROC SQL;
    CREATE TABLE TWO AS    ❶
    SELECT *    ❷
    FROM SQL_TEST
    GROUP BY SUBJECT
    HAVING COUNT(SUBJECT) = 2;    ❸
QUIT;
```

This program adds a CREATE TABLE statement ❶ so that a new data set will be created, rather than a listing. All you want in this new data set is a list of subject numbers corresponding to all subjects with exactly two observations. Therefore, you don't really need the NUMBER variable in the new data set. This is why it was omitted from the SELECT statement. You will also notice that an asterisk is used in the SELECT statement instead of a list of variables. The asterisk is a shorthand way of asking for all the variables in the data set to be listed in the FROM clause. Finally, the HAVING clause ❸ is used (instead of a WHERE clause) whenever the query includes a statistical function such as COUNT. To verify that the newly created data set (TWO) really contains what you want, a listing from a PROC PRINT is shown next:

```
Listing of Data Set TWO

SUBJECT       DAY        X      Y      Z

   1        MONDAY      10     20     30
   1        FRIDAY      11     21     31
   4        FRIDAY      40     50     60
   4        SATURDAY    41     42      .
   7        THURSDAY    14      .     22
   7        MONDAY      10     13     14
```

You may want to use PROC SQL to create a small data set consisting only of subject numbers corresponding to those subjects with exactly two observations. To do this, all you have to do is modify Program 6-4, including only the variable name SUBJECT in the SELECT statement.

Using PROC SQL to Create a Macro Variable

One useful feature of PROC SQL is its ability to create macro variables. For example, with one SQL query, you can create a macro variable containing a list of subject numbers which can, in turn, be used with an IN comparison operator to subset a data set. In Program 6-5, you see how Program 6-4 can be modified to create a macro variable containing the list of subject numbers with exactly two observations.

Program 6-5: Using PROC SQL to Create a Macro Variable Containing a List of Subject Numbers for Subjects with Exactly Two Observations

```
PROC SQL NOPRINT;    ❶
    SELECT QUOTE(SUBJECT)    ❷
    INTO :SUBJ_LIST SEPARATED BY " "    ❸
    FROM SQL_TEST
    GROUP BY SUBJECT
    HAVING COUNT(SUBJECT) = 2;
QUIT;
```

The key to this process is the INTO clause ❸, which instructs the SQL query to create a macro variable. Line ❶ includes the NOPRINT option since we neither want to create a data set nor to produce a listing of the resulting query. The SELECT statement ❷ uses the QUOTE function since the goal is to have each of the subject numbers in quotes (so it can be used later as part of an IN comparison operator). An IN comparison operator, when used with a character variable, can be a list of quoted values separated by either spaces or commas. Spaces were chosen here. If you prefer commas, simply modify line ❸ by placing a comma between the double quotes, instead of a space. (If SUBJECT was a numeric variable, you would not use the QUOTE function—the IN operator used with numeric variables consists of a list of numbers separated by either spaces or commas.) The remainder of the program has been explained previously.

The macro variable SUBJ_LIST is the text string:

```
"1" "4" "7"
```

An example of how this macro variable could be used is shown in Program 6-6.

Program 6-6: Demonstrating How to Use the Previously Generated Macro Variable

```
PROC PRINT DATA=SQL_TEST;
    WHERE SUBJECT IN (&SUBJ_LIST);
    TITLE "Subset of Subjects with Exactly Two Observations";
    ID SUBJECT;
RUN;
```

The result is a listing of all patients with exactly two visits:

```
Subset of Subjects with Exactly Two Observations

SUBJECT        DAY          X     Y     Z

   1         MONDAY        10    20    30
   1         FRIDAY        11    21    31
   4         FRIDAY        40    50    60
   4         SATURDAY      41    42     .
   7         MONDAY        10    13    14
   7         THURSDAY      14     .    22
```

Using a Summary Function to Compute Group Means

Another summary function, besides the COUNT function that you have used above, is the AVG function that computes means (averages). Without a GROUP BY clause, the AVG function will return a mean of all observations; with a GROUP BY clause, you can compute means for each level of the GROUP BY variable. Program 6-7 uses the AVG function to compute the mean value of X for each subject.

Program 6-7: Using the AVG Function to Compute Subject Means

```
PROC SQL;
   SELECT SUBJECT, X,
          AVG(X) AS AVE_X
   FROM SQL_TEST
   GROUP BY SUBJECT;
QUIT;
```

Here the mean value of X is computed and given the variable name AVE_X as requested. The result is shown next:

SUBJECT	X	AVE_X
1	10	10.5
1	11	10.5
2	30	30
3	14	12.66667
3	13	12.66667
3	11	12.66667
4	40	40.5
4	41	40.5
5	8	6.333333
5	6	6.333333
5	5	6.333333
7	14	12
7	10	12

You can write an SQL query that combines this average value with the original scores. For example, you might want to see each subject's value for X expressed as a percentage of the average of the X's for that subject. For example, subject 1 has two values of X (10 and 11) with the average being 10.5. The value of 10 is 5% below this subject's average X. Program 6-8 shows the code to accomplish these calculations.

Program 6-8: Computing a Percentage Change for Each Subject

```
PROC SQL;
   SELECT SUBJECT, X,
          AVG(X) AS AVE_X,
          100 * (X - CALCULATED AVE_X)/X AS PERCENT_X
   FROM SQL_TEST
   GROUP BY SUBJECT;
QUIT;
```

First, the variable AVE_X is created using the AVG function. In the same SELECT statement, this newly created variable is used in an arithmetic statement to compute the percentage value, which is given the name PERCENT_X. The keyword CALCULATED precedes the name AVE_X to show that this variable is computed by PROC SQL. The result is

```
Subset of Subjects with Exactly Two Observations

SUBJECT          X      AVE_X   PERCENT_X

1               10       10.5          -5
1               11       10.5    4.545455
2               30         30           0
3               14   12.66667     9.52381
3               13   12.66667    2.564103
3               11   12.66667    -15.1515
4               40       40.5       -1.25
4               41       40.5    1.219512
5                8   6.333333    20.83333
5                6   6.333333    -5.55556
5                5   6.333333    -26.6667
7               14         12    14.28571
7               10         12         -20
```

As you can see, PROC SQL is very powerful and can accomplish amazing feats. The decision of when to use PROC SQL versus a DATA or PROC step approach may be a function of what you are most familiar with or, possibly, efficiency considerations. There is no way to give you a rule of thumb for when to use PROC SQL and when to use alternative approaches. For small data sets, the choice will most likely come down to which method you use the most and with which you are most comfortable. When working with large data sets, it may be necessary to try out each method on some sample data to determine which will use less time or system resources.

Restructuring SAS Data Sets Using Arrays

Introduction

One approach to working with longitudinal data sets is to restructure the data set—either going from one observation per subject (or other unit of analysis) to several or vice versa. For example, you may have several diagnosis codes in a single observation (visit) and want to compute frequencies of each possible diagnosis code. To do this, you will find it more convenient to have one observation for each diagnosis code, resulting in possibly several observations per subject. On the other hand, you may have several observations per subject and want to make lots of comparisons between observations. Placing all the information for a single subject in a single observation usually makes this process much easier.

This chapter shows you how to accomplish these goals using arrays in a SAS DATA step. Chapter 8 demonstrates how this is done using PROC TRANSPOSE.

Creating a New Data Set with Several Observations per Subject from a Data Set with One Observation per Subject

Suppose you have a data set called DIAGNOSE, with the variables PATNO (patient number) and DATE (date of visit) and three diagnosis codes, DX1, DX2, and DX3. You can run Program 7-1 to create a test data set.

Program 7-1: Creating the DIAGNOSE Data Set

```
DATA DIAGNOSE;
    INPUT @1  PATNO     2.
          @3  DATE       MMDDYY10.
          @14 DX1 - DX3;
    FORMAT DATE MMDDYY10.;
DATALINES;
1 10/21/1999 1 2 .
2 10/29/1999 2 . .
3 11/11/2000 3 . .
4 01/01/2000 1 2 3
5 02/02/2000 3 2 .
6 03/15/2000 4 . .
;
```

The observations in the data set DIAGNOSE are shown next:

```
Listing of Data Set DIAGNOSE

Obs    PATNO        DATE       DX1    DX2    DX3

  1      1      10/21/1999      1      2      .
  2      2      10/29/1999      2      .      .
  3      3      11/11/2000      3      .      .
  4      4      01/01/2000      1      2      3
  5      5      02/02/2000      3      2      .
  6      6      03/15/2000      4      .      .
```

As you can see, some subjects have only one diagnosis code, some two, and some all three. Suppose you want to count how many subjects have diagnosis 1, how many have diagnosis 2, and so on. You don't care if the diagnosis code is listed as DX1, DX2, or DX3. In the example here, you would have a frequency of two for diagnosis code 1, a frequency of four for diagnosis code 2, a frequency of three for diagnosis code 3, and a frequency of one for diagnosis code 4.

One way to accomplish this task is to transform the data set DIAGNOSE, which has one observation per subject and three diagnosis variables, to a data set that has a single diagnosis variable and as many observations per subject as there are diagnoses for that subject. This new data set (call it NEW_DX) would look like the one shown next:

```
Listing of Data Set NEW_DX

PATNO     DX

  1        1
  1        2
  2        2
  3        3
  4        1
  4        2
  4        3
  5        3
  5        2
  6        4
```

Using the data set NEW_DX, it is now a simple job to count diagnosis codes using PROC FREQ on the single variable DX. Let us first write a SAS DATA step that creates the data set NEW_DX from the data set DIAGNOSE but does not use arrays. The code is shown in Program 7-2.

Program 7-2: Creating Multiple Observations from a Single Observation without Using an Array

```
DATA NEW_DX;
   SET DIAGNOSE (DROP = DATE);   ❶

   DX = DX1;
   IF DX NE . THEN OUTPUT;   ❷
   DX = DX2;
   IF DX NE . THEN OUTPUT;   ❸
   DX = DX3;
   IF DX NE . THEN OUTPUT;   ❹

   KEEP PATNO DX;
RUN;
```

Let's see how this program works. As you read in each observation from the data set DIAGNOSE, you create from one to three observations in the new data set NEW_DX. The SET statement ❶ brings in each observation from the original data set (DIAGNOSE), one at a time. In the first iteration of this DATA step, the values of PATNO, DX1, DX2, and DX3 are 1, 1, 2, and missing, respectively. Next, a new variable, DX, is set equal to DX1 (which is a 1). Since this is not a missing value, the OUTPUT statement ❷ is executed and the first observation in the data set NEW_DX is formed. The values of all the variables in the PDV (program data vector, the place where variables are stored during the DATA step) at this point are

```
PATNO=1    DX1=1    DX2=2    DX3=.    DX=1
```

Since we have a KEEP statement in the DATA step, only the values for PATNO and DX are written out to the new data set. Next, the value of DX is set to DX2 (which is a 2). Again, since the value of DX is not a missing value, another observation is written to the data set NEW_DX ❸. Finally, DX is set equal to DX3 (which is a missing value). Since the following IF statement is not true, the third OUTPUT statement of the DATA step ❸ does not execute and execution returns to the top of the DATA step and another observation from the data set DIAGNOSE is read. As you can see, the program will create as many observations per subject as there are nonmissing DX codes for that subject.

Notice the repetitive nature of the program and your array lightbulb should turn on. Program 7-3 accomplishes the same goal but uses arrays.

Program 7-3: Creating Multiple Observations from a Single Observation Using an Array

```
DATA NEW_DX;
    SET DIAGNOSE (DROP = DATE);
    ARRAY DXARRAY[3] DX1 - DX3;    ❶

    DO I = 1 TO 3;
        DX = DXARRAY[I];
        IF DX NE . THEN OUTPUT;
    END;

    KEEP PATNO DX;
RUN;
```

In this program, you first create an array called DXARRAY, which contains the three numeric variables DX1, DX2, and DX3 ❶. Using an array allows you to refer to any of the variables associated with it by listing the array name, subscripted with the appropriate index (subscript). Also, subscripted array elements exist only in the DATA step in which they are created and they are not part of the SAS data set being created. Finally, array names follow the same rules as SAS variable names. (**Note:** Do not use the same name for an array as a variable in your data set—it can cause unpredictable results.)

Now back to the program. The two lines of code inside the DO loop are similar to the repeated lines in the nonarray example (Program 7-2) with the variable names DX1, DX2, and DX3 replaced by the array elements.

To count the number of subjects with each diagnosis code, you can now use PROC FREQ like this:

```
PROC FREQ DATA=NEW_DX;
   TABLES DX / NOCUM;
RUN;
```

In this example, by using an array, you only saved one line of SAS code. However, if there were more variables, DX1 to DX50 for example, the savings would be substantial.

Another Example of Creating Multiple Observations from a Single Observation

Here is an example that is similar to the previous one. You start with a data set that contains an ID variable and three variables S1, S2, and S3, which represent a score at times 1, 2, and 3, respectively. The original data set called ONEPER can be created by running Program 7-4.

Program 7-4: Creating the Sample Data Set ONEPER

```
DATA ONEPER;
   INPUT ID $ S1-S3;
DATALINES;
01 3 4 5
02 7 8 9
03 6 5 4
;
```

A listing of the data set ONEPER is shown below:

```
Listing of Data Set ONEPER

Obs    ID    S1    S2    S3

 1     01     3     4     5
 2     02     7     8     9
 3     03     6     5     4
```

You want to create a new data set called MANYPER, which looks like this:

```
Data Set MANYPER

ID    TIME    SCORE
01     1       3
01     2       4
01     3       5
02     1       7
02     2       8
02     3       9
03     1       6
03     2       5
03     3       4
```

That is, instead of one observation per subject containing three scores, you want three observations per subject with one score each (and a variable called TIME to tell which of the three scores it represents). The program to transform the data set ONEPER to the data set MANYPER is similar to Program 7-3 except that you need to create the TIME variable in the transformed data set. This is easily accomplished by naming the DO loop counter TIME as shown in Program 7-5.

Program 7-5: Creating Multiple Observations from a Single Observation Using an Array

```
DATA MANYPER;
   SET ONEPER;
   ARRAY S[3];    ❶

   DO TIME = 1 TO 3;    ❷
      SCORE = S[TIME];
      OUTPUT;
   END;

   KEEP ID TIME SCORE;
RUN;
```

You first notice that the ARRAY statement ❶ in this DATA step does not have a variable list. This was done to demonstrate another way of writing an ARRAY statement. When the variable list is omitted, the variable names default to the array name followed by the numbers from the lower bound to the upper bound. In this case, the statement

```
ARRAYS[3];
```

is equivalent to

```
ARRAY S[3] S1-S3;
```

The SET statement brings in observations from the data set ONEPER, which contains the variables ID, S1, S2, and S3. This program is similar to the previous program except that the DO loop variable is called TIME ❷, and you always output three observations for every observation in the data set ONEPER. (If there are any missing values for the variables S1, S2, and S3, there will be an observation in the new data set with a missing value for the variable called SCORE.)

Let's extend this program to include an additional dimension.

Going from One Observation per Subject to Many Observations per Subject Using Multidimensional Arrays

Suppose you have a SAS data set (call it WT_ONE) that contains an ID and six weights for each subject in an experiment. The first three values represent weights at times 1, 2, and 3 under condition 1; the next three values represent weights at times 1, 2, and 3 under condition 2 (see the diagram below):

CONDITION					
1			2		
TIME			TIME		
1	2	3	1	2	3
WT1	WT2	WT3	WT4	WT5	WT6

To clarify this, suppose the data set WT_ONE contains two observations:

```
Data Set WT_ONE

ID    WT1   WT2   WT3   WT4   WT5   WT6
01    155   158   162   149   148   147
02    110   112   114   107   108   109
```

Here, weights 1, 2, and 3 correspond to measurements made under condition 1 at times 1 to 3, and weights 4, 5, and 6 correspond to measurements made under condition 2 at times 1 to 3. You want a new data set called WT_MANY to look like this:

```
Data Set WT_MANY

ID      COND      TIME      WEIGHT
01      1         1         155
01      1         2         158
01      1         3         162
01      2         1         149
01      2         2         148
01      2         3         147
02      1         1         110
02      1         2         112
02      1         3         114
02      2         1         107
02      2         2         108
02      2         3         109
```

A convenient way to make this conversion is to create a two-dimensional array with the first dimension representing condition and the second representing time. So instead of having a one-dimensional array like this

```
ARRAY WEIGHT[6] WT1-WT6;
```

you could create a two-dimensional array like this:

```
ARRAY WEIGHT[2,3] WT1-WT6;
```

The comma between the 2 and 3 separates the dimensions of the array. This is a 2 (rows) by 3 (columns) array. The array element WEIGHT[2,3], for example, would represent a subject's weight under condition 2 at time 3.

Let's use this array structure to create the new data set, which contains six observations for each ID. Each observation is to contain the ID and one of the six weights, along with two new variables, COND and TIME, which represent the condition and the time at which the weight was recorded. Program 7-6 demonstrates how a multidimensional array can be used.

Program 7-6: Using a Multidimensional Array to Restructure a Data Set

```
DATA WT_MANY;
   SET WT_ONE;

   ARRAY WTS [2,3] WT1-WT6;
   DO COND = 1 TO 2;
      DO TIME = 1 TO 3;
         WEIGHT = WTS[COND,TIME];
         OUTPUT;
      END;
   END;

   DROP WT1-WT6;
RUN;
```

To cover all combinations of condition and time, you use "nested" DO loops—that is, a DO loop within a DO loop. Here's how it works: COND is first set to 1 by the outer loop. Next, TIME is set to 1, 2, and 3 in the inner loop while COND remains at 1. Once the inner loop is completed, (TIME has reached 3), the control returns to the outer loop where condition (COND) is now set to 2, and the inner loop cycles through three times again. Each time a COND and TIME combination is selected, a WEIGHT is set equal to the appropriate array element and the observation is written out to the new data set.

Demonstrating the Use of a Multidimensional Array

It's now time to reverse the transformation process. Program 7-7 reverses the process demonstrated by Program 7-3—showing how to create a single observation from multiple observations. You might want to use this transformation when you need to compute differences between observations and would rather have all the values for a single subject in one observation.

This time you will start with the data set MANYPER and create the data set ONEPER. First the program, then the explanation:

Program 7-7: Creating a Data Set with One Observation per Subject from a Data Set with Multiple Observations per Subject

```
***Caution, this program will not work if there are any missing
   time values.;

PROC SORT DATA=MANYPER;     ❶
   BY ID TIME;
RUN;

DATA ONEPER;

   ARRAY S[3] S1-S3;    ❷
   RETAIN S1-S3;        ❸

   SET MANYPER;
   BY ID;

   S[TIME] = SCORE;
   IF LAST.ID = 1 THEN OUTPUT;    ❹

   KEEP ID S1-S3;
RUN;
```

First, you sort the data set MANYPER to be sure that the observations are in ID and TIME order ❶. In this example, the data set MANYPER is already in the correct order, but the SORT procedure makes the program more general. Next, you need to create an array containing the variables you want in the ONEPER data set, namely, S1, S2, and S3 ❷. You can "play computer" to see how this program works. The first observation in the data set MANYPER is

```
   ID = 01    TIME = 1     SCORE = 4
```

Since TIME is equal to 1, S[TIME] is equivalent to S[1], which represents the variable S1 and is set to the value of SCORE, which is 4. Since LAST.ID is false, the OUTPUT statement ❹ does not execute and control returns to the top of the DATA step. The value of S1 is still equal to 4 since it is one of the retained variables (as are the variables S2 and S3, because of the RETAIN statement ❸ that follows the ARRAY statement). The values of retained variables are not set to a missing value for each iteration of the DATA step as are the values of nonretained variables.

In the next observation TIME is 2 and SCORE is 5, so the variable S2 is assigned a value of 5. Finally, the third and last observation is read for ID 01. S3 is set to the value of SCORE, which is 6, and since LAST.ID is true, the first observation in the data set ONEPER is written. Everything seems fine. Almost.

What if the data set MANYPER did not have an observation at all three values of TIME for each ID? To see what happens when there is a missing value, look at the data set (MANYPER2) shown below:

```
Data Set MANYPER2

ID    TIME    SCORE
01     1        3
01     2        4
01     3        5
02     1        7
02     3        9
03     1        6
03     2        5
03     3        4
```

Notice that ID number 02 does not have an observation with TIME = 2. What will happen if you run Program 7-7? Since you retained the values of S1, S2, and S3 and never replaced the value of S2 for ID number 02, ID number 2 will be given the value of S2 from the previous subject! This is not what you want. You must always be careful when you retain variables. To be sure that this will not happen, you need to set the values of S1, S2, and S3 to missing each time you encounter a new subject. This is easily accomplished by initializing each of the new variables to a missing value each time a new subject is encountered (FIRST.ID is true). Program 7-8 shows the corrected program.

Program 7-8: Creating a Data Set with One Observation per Subject from a Data Set with Multiple Observations per Subject (Corrected Version)

```
PROC SORT DATA=MANYPER2;
   BY ID TIME;
RUN;

DATA ONEPER;

   ARRAY S[3] S1-S3;
   RETAIN S1-S3;
```

```
   SET MANYPER2;
   BY ID;

   IF FIRST.ID = 1 THEN DO I = 1 TO  3;
      S[I] = .;
      END;

   S[TIME] = SCORE;
   IF LAST.ID = 1 THEN OUTPUT;

   KEEP ID S1-S3;
RUN;
```

This program now works correctly whether or not there are missing TIME values.

An Alternative Program

An interesting alternative to Program 7-8 was suggested by Robert Virgile, author of *An Array of Challenges: Test Your SAS Skills*. It is somewhat complicated, so feel free to skip it if you want. It is shown in Program 7-9, followed by a brief explanation.

Program 7-9: Demonstrating an Alternative to Program 7-8 That Does Not Need to Initialize Variables

```
PROC SORT DATA=MANYPER2;
   BY ID TIME;
RUN;

DATA ONEPER;
   ARRAY S[3] S1-S3;
   DO I = 1 TO 3 UNTIL (LAST.ID);     ❶
      SET MANYPER2;     ❷
      BY ID;
      S[TIME] = SCORE;
      IF LAST.ID = 1 THEN OUTPUT;
   END;
   KEEP ID S1-S3;
RUN;
```

The reason this program does not have to initialize (set to missing) the variables S1, S2, and S3 is that the SAS DATA step does that for you. Since the SET statement ❷ is *inside* the DO loop, you do not need to retain the variables S1, S2, and S3—they are reset to missing only when the DATA step iterates. Variables coming from a SET statement are automatically retained. Therefore, as long as you are within the DO loop, reading in observations from the data set MANYPER, the values of S1, S2, and S3 get assigned their values, and they are not set back to missing. Once you finish with the DO loop, you return to the top of the DATA step where the variables S1, S2, and S3 are set to missing as usual. The UNTIL clause added to the DO loop ❶ stops the loop prematurely if there are fewer than three observations for an ID (that is when LAST.ID is true).

Another Example of a Multidimensional Array

This example is the reverse of Program 7-6. That is, you want to start from the data set WT_MANY and wind up with the data set WT_ONE. The solution to this problem is similar to Program 7-8, except you use a multidimensional array. Note, however, that the solution presented in Program 7-10 works whether or not there are any missing observations in the data set.

Program 7-10: Creating a Data Set with One Observation per Subject from a Data Set with Multiple Observations per Subject Using a Multidimensional Array

```
PROC SORT DATA=WT_MANY;
   BY ID COND TIME;
RUN;

DATA WT_ONE;

   ARRAY WT[2,3] WT1-WT6;
   RETAIN WT1-WT6;

   SET WT_MANY;
   BY ID;

   IF FIRST.ID = 1 THEN
   DO I = 1 TO  2;
      DO J = 1 TO 3;
         WT[I,J] = .;
      END;
   END;
```

```
   WT[COND,TIME] = WEIGHT;
   IF LAST.ID = 1 THEN OUTPUT;

   KEEP ID WT1-WT6;
RUN;
```

Again, notice the similarities between this program and Program 7-8. First, each time you process a new subject, you initialize all of the WT variables to a missing value (using nested DO loops). Next, depending on the value of COND and TIME, set the appropriate WT to the value of the variable WEIGHT. Finally, when you reach the last observation for a subject, output the single observation, keeping only the variables ID and WT1-WT6.

You will find times when it is more convenient to have all the observations per subject in one observation and times when you need each measurement taken on a subject in a separate observation. For those readers who use PROC ANOVA or PROC GLM, the decision of which structure is more convenient could depend on whether or not you plan to use a REPEATED statement (one observation per subject), or if you want to write a MODEL statement including all the repeated measure factors (many observations per subject).

Restructuring SAS Data Sets Using PROC TRANSPOSE

Introduction

Chapter 7 described how to restructure SAS data sets using DATA step programming. This is usually the most flexible way to get the job done. However, PROC TRANSPOSE was designed specifically to perform one-to-many and many-to-one transformations. This author usually reverts back to the comfort of the DATA step—doing what most people do, using what they are most comfortable with. There are occasions when PROC TRANSPOSE is much easier and quicker.

Most of the examples in Chapter 7 will be redone here using PROC TRANSPOSE. You will see where each method has its advantages, and you can make your own decisions about where and when to use either method.

Going from One Observation to Several Observations

Using the same DIAGNOSE data set from the last chapter (see Program 7-1), you start with almost the world's simplest PROC TRANSPOSE program. Since you want to turn rows into columns for each patient ID, you must first sort the data set by PATNO and then use PATNO as a BY variable in the TRANSPOSE procedure. When a BY variable is used with PROC TRANSPOSE, the BY variable is not transposed, and the row-by-column transformation occurs only within each BY variable. Program 8-1 demonstrates how this works.

Program 8-1: Going from One Observation to Several Using PROC TRANSPOSE

```
PROC SORT DATA=DIAGNOSE;    ❶
   BY PATNO;
RUN;


PROC TRANSPOSE DATA=DIAGNOSE OUT=DX_COUNT;    ❷
   BY PATNO;
   VAR DX1-DX3;
RUN;
```

In its simplest form, PROC TRANSPOSE has an input data set specified by the DATA= procedure option and an output data set specified by the OUT= procedure option. Since you only want the DX codes in the new data set, you place the variable names DX1-DX3 in the VAR statement. The listing of the data set DX_COUNT is almost what you want:

```
Listing of Data Set DX_COUNT

Obs      PATNO     _NAME_     COL1

  1        1        DX1        1
  2        1        DX2        2
  3        1        DX3        .
  4        2        DX1        2
  5        2        DX2        .
  6        2        DX3        .
  7        3        DX1        3
  8        3        DX2        .
  9        3        DX3        .
 10        4        DX1        1
 11        4        DX2        2
 12        4        DX3        3
 13        5        DX1        3
 14        5        DX2        2
 15        5        DX3        .
 16        6        DX1        4
 17        6        DX2        .
 18        6        DX3        .
```

Inspection of the DX_COUNT data set shows that within each patient number (PATNO), the original variables DX1, DX2, and DX3 have become rows in the new data set. The procedure-generated variable names _NAME_ and COL1 represent the original VAR names and the new name for the column variable. It would be nice to fancy up this data set a bit by getting rid of the _NAME_ variable and renaming COL1 to DX. This is easily done by a slight modification to the PROC statements as shown in Program 8-2.

Program 8-2: Modifying the PROC TRANSPOSE Statement to Drop _NAME_ and Rename COL1

```
PROC TRANSPOSE DATA=DIAGNOSE OUT=DX_COUNT(RENAME=(COL1=DX)
               DROP=_NAME_);
   BY PATNO;
   VAR DX1-DX3;
RUN;
```

The RENAME= data set option is used to rename COL1 to DX, and the DROP= data set option eliminates the _NAME_ variable. The output is now closer to what you want:

```
Listing of Data Set DX_COUNT

Obs      PATNO      DX

  1        1         1
  2        1         2
  3        1         .
  4        2         2
  5        2         .
  6        2         .
  7        3         3
  8        3         .
  9        3         .
 10        4         1
 11        4         2
 12        4         3
 13        5         3
 14        5         2
 15        5         .
 16        6         4
 17        6         .
 18        6         .
```

All that is left to do is to eliminate the observations with a missing value for DX. This is accomplished by adding a WHERE data set option to the output data set as in Program 8-3.

Program 8-3: Eliminating the Observations with Missing Values for DX

```
PROC TRANSPOSE DATA=DIAGNOSE
               OUT=DX_COUNT(RENAME=(COL1=DX) WHERE=(DX NE .)
               DROP=_NAME_);
   BY PATNO;
   VAR DX1-DX3;
RUN;
```

All that was added to Program 8-3 was the WHERE= data set option, selecting observations only when the DX code is not missing. There is no need to show the resulting output data set. It is the same as the previous listing, except that the observations with a missing DX code are no longer present.

Another Example of Creating Multiple Observations from a Single Observation

This example uses the data set created by Program 7-4. As you may recall, each subject (ID) has three variables, S1, S2, and S3, which represent scores at times 1, 2, and 3, respectively. Using PROC TRANSPOSE for this example creates an interesting problem and a novel solution. You start out in a similar manner to Program 8-3.

Program 8-4: Creating the Data Set ONEPER and Transforming It into a Data Set with Several Observations per Subject

```
DATA ONEPER;
   INFORMAT ID $2.;
   INPUT ID S1 S2 S3;
DATALINES;
01     3      4      5
02     7      8      9
03     6      5      4
RUN;
PROC SORT DATA=ONEPER;
   BY ID;
RUN;
```

```
PROC TRANSPOSE DATA=ONEPER OUT=TEMP(RENAME=(COL1=SCORE));
    BY ID;
RUN;
```

This all looks straightforward. However, as you can see in the listing below, everything is fine except that you don't have a variable called TIME with the appropriate values. It is easy to rename _NAME_ to TIME, but you also need to change the values S1, S2, and S3 to the numerical values 1, 2, and 3. First, have a look at the listing, and then we'll fix the time problem:

```
Listing of Data Set TEMP

Obs     ID     _NAME_     SCORE

 1      01      S1          3
 2      01      S2          4
 3      01      S3          5
 4      02      S1          7
 5      02      S2          8
 6      02      S3          9
 7      03      S1          6
 8      03      S2          5
 9      03      S3          4
```

Program 8-5: Converting the Values of _NAME_ to TIME Values

```
DATA MANYPER;
    SET TEMP;
    TIME = INPUT(COMPRESS(_NAME_,"S"),8.);   ❶
    DROP _NAME_;
RUN;
```

You need to convert the values of S1, S2, and S3 to the numbers 1, 2, and 3. First, you need to get rid of the "S." There are several approaches to this problem, but using the COMPRESS function works quite well. If you compress the "S" from the values, you are left with the characters "1," "2," and "3." The COMPRESS function removes all characters listed in the second argument ("S," in this example) from the string identified in the first argument (_NAME_).

The INPUT function then performs the character-to-numeric conversion, and the values of the new variable TIME are the numbers 1, 2, and 3. Reviewing the INPUT function, you specify the character variable to convert as the first argument and a numeric informat as the second argument. The informat you choose can be larger than the numeral you are converting, as in this example.

The listing below verifies that this program worked as designed:

```
Listing of Data Set MANYPER

Obs    ID    SCORE    TIME

 1     01      3       1
 2     01      4       2
 3     01      5       3
 4     02      7       1
 5     02      8       2
 6     02      9       3
 7     03      6       1
 8     03      5       2
 9     03      4       3
```

Going from One Observation per Subject to Many Observations per Subject

This is the final example of using PROC TRANSPOSE to go from one observation per subject to many observations per subject. Again, this example follows the identical problem you tackled in Chapter 7 using DATA step approaches. Each subject (ID) is measured six times, the first three values represent the weights at times 1, 2, and 3 under condition 1; the next three values represent the weights at times 1, 2, and 3 under condition 2.

Program 8-6: Going from One Observation per Subject to Many Observations per Subject Using PROC TRANSPOSE

```
DATA WT_ONE;
    INFORMAT ID $2.;
    INPUT ID WT1-WT6;
DATALINES;
01    155    158    162    149    148    147
02    110    112    114    107    108    109
RUN;
PROC SORT DATA=WT_ONE;
   BY ID;
RUN;

PROC TRANSPOSE DATA=WT_ONE OUT=WT_COND1(RENAME=(COL1=WEIGHT));
   BY ID;
   VAR WT1-WT6;
RUN;
```

The SORT and TRANSFORM steps are fairly straightforward. However, if you inspect the listing that follows, you will see that you are not quite there. Here is a listing of the data set WT_COND1:

```
Listing of Data Set WT_COND1

Obs     ID     _NAME_     WEIGHT

 1      01      WT1         155
 2      01      WT2         158
 3      01      WT3         162
 4      01      WT4         149
 5      01      WT5         148
 6      01      WT6         147
 7      02      WT1         110
 8      02      WT2         112
 9      02      WT3         114
10      02      WT4         107
11      02      WT5         108
12      02      WT6         109
```

You want to create two variables (COND and TIME) from the single variable _NAME_. When _NAME_ has the value WT1, WT2, or WT3, the value of COND should be 1, and the values of TIME should be 1, 2, and 3. For WT4, WT5, and WT6, COND should be 2, and TIME should cycle from 1 to 3 again. The short DATA step in Program 8-7 does just that.

Program 8-7: Adding the Final DATA Step to Create the COND and TIME Variables

```
DATA WT_MANY;
   SET WT_COND1;
   TIME = INPUT(COMPRESS(_NAME_,"WT"),8.);
   IF TIME LE 3 THEN COND = 1;
   ELSE DO;
      COND = 2;
      TIME = TIME - 3;
   END;
   DROP _NAME_;
RUN;
```

The same technique you used in Program 8-5 is used here. The COMPRESS function removes the "W" and "T" from the value, and the numerals are converted to numbers using the INPUT function.

Some simple DATA step logic ensures that the proper values of COND and TIME are computed. The final listing of this data set matches the one in Chapter 7. Here is a case where the DATA step approach was probably easier than the PROC TRANSPOSE approach.

```
Listing of Data Set WT_MANY

Obs    ID      WEIGHT    TIME    COND

  1    01       155       1       1
  2    01       158       2       1
  3    01       162       3       1
  4    01       149       1       2
  5    01       148       2       2
  6    01       147       3       2
  7    02       110       1       1
  8    02       112       2       1
  9    02       114       3       1
 10    02       107       1       2
 11    02       108       2       2
 12    02       109       3       2
```

Creating a Data Set with One Observation per Subject from a Data Set with Multiple Observations per Subject

Following the outline of Chapter 7, let's now try to take a data set with several observations per subject and create a data set with only one observation per subject. Let's start with the data set MANYPER, which you can create by running several of the programs described earlier in this chapter, or more easily, by running Program 8-8.

Program 8-8: Creating the Data Set MANYPER

```
DATA MANYPER;
INFORMAT ID $2.;
   INPUT ID $ TIME SCORE;
DATALINES;
01    1     3
01    2     4
01    3     5
02    1     7
02    2     8
02    3     9
03    1     6
```

```
03      2       5
03      3       4
RUN;
```

The PROC TRANSPOSE statements to transform this data set into one with a single observation per subject are shown in Program 8-9.

Program 8-9: Transforming a Data Set with Several Observations per Subject into a Data Set with One Observation per Subject

```
***Note: This program ONLY works correctly if there are no
         missing TIME values;
PROC SORT DATA=MANYPER;
   BY ID TIME;
RUN;

PROC TRANSPOSE DATA=MANYPER OUT=ONEPER(DROP=_NAME_) PREFIX=S;    ❶
   BY ID;
   VAR SCORE;
RUN;
```

Since you want one observation per subject (ID), you first need to sort by ID (and TIME just to be safe). Line ❶ uses the PREFIX= procedure option. Instead of the default variable names COL1, COL2, etc. that PROC TRANSPOSE uses for the new column variables, you can specify a prefix to replace the "COL" as part of the variable names. Here the letter "S" was used. Since there were three observations for each ID, the new data set ONEPER now has three variables S1, S2, and S3 (instead of COL1, COL2, and COL3, which you would have gotten without the PREFIX= option). A listing of the data set ONEPER follows:

```
Listing of Data Set ONEPER

Obs    ID     S1    S2    S3

 1     01     3     4     5
 2     02     7     8     9
 3     03     6     5     4
```

That certainly looks easier than the DATA step approach you saw in Chapter 7. However, a problem arises if all TIME values are not present in the MANYPER data set. To demonstrate this, run Program 8-10 to create the data set MANYPER2, which is missing a time 2 value for ID number two.

Program 8-10: Creating the Data Set MANYPER2 (Which Is Missing TIME=2 for ID=02)

```
DATA MANYPER2;
    INFORMAT ID $2.;
    INPUT ID TIME SCORE;
DATALINES;
01          1          3
01          2          4
01          3          5
02          1          7
02          3          9
03          1          6
03          2          5
03          3          4
RUN;
```

Let's see what happens when you run Program 8-9 (with the data set MANYPER2 instead of MANYPER). Look at the listing below:

```
Listing of Data Set ONEPER2

Obs    ID    S1    S2    S3

 1     01     3     4     5
 2     02     7     9     .
 3     03     6     5     4
```

See what happened? The score for ID=2, TIME=3 appears as S2 instead of S3, and the value for S3 is missing. That is, the three values for S1, S2, and S3 for ID=2 should have been 7, missing, and 9. There are probably some applications where this result would be just fine. In this example, you have an association between the variable names S1, S2, and S3 and the three times. There are several ways to fix this problem. The easiest way is to include an ID statement as shown in Program 8-11.

Program 8-11: Fixing the Program by Using an ID Statement

```
PROC TRANSPOSE DATA=MANYPER2 OUT=ONEPER(DROP=_NAME_) PREFIX=S;
   BY ID;
   ID TIME;
   VAR SCORE;
RUN;
```

The ID statement uses the values of the ID variable (TIME, in this case) added to the PREFIX value (S), to produce the names of the column variables. Since TIME has values of 1, 2, and 3, the column names become S1, S2, and S3.

When you include a BY, ID, and VAR statement in PROC TRANSPOSE, you can think of the ID variable, in combination with the PREFIX value, becoming the *columns* of the output data set, the BY variable becoming the *rows* of the output data set, and the variable listed in the VAR statement becoming the *contents of the cells* of the output data set. Inspect the listings of the data sets MANYPER2 and ONEPER to verify that this is the case:

```
Listing of Data Set MANYPER2        Listing of Data Set ONEPER

Obs    ID    TIME    SCORE          Obs    ID    S1    S2    S3

1      01     1        3            1      01     3     4     5
2      01     2        4            2      02     7     .     9
3      01     3        5            3      03     6     5     4
4      02     1        7
5      02     3        9
6      03     1        6
7      03     2        5
8      03     3        4
```

Now that you have seen the capabilities of PROC TRANSPOSE, each time you need to transform a SAS data set, you have a choice of using PROC TRANSPOSE or a DATA step approach. Depending on the situation, one method may be easier than the other. Or, you may just feel more comfortable with one of the methods. That's OK.

Study One: Operations on a Clinical Database

Introduction

This is the first of the applications chapters. Although the examples presented here pertain to a fictitious data set of clinical encounters, the techniques that are developed have wide application to any situation where you have multiple observations on a single subject or unit of analysis.

Description of the Clinical Data Set

All of the examples in this chapter are based on a small set of patient visits to a clinic. The number of observations was kept small so that you can verify all the results by inspection of the output listings. The variables PATIENT (patient number), VISIT_DATE, GENDER, and STATE need no explanation. The three variables HR, SBP, and DBP represent heart rate (in beats per minute), systolic blood pressure, and diastolic blood pressure. The variables DX1, DX2, and DX3 represent up to three diagnosis codes relating to the current visit (see the PROC FORMAT for code descriptions). The variable VITAMINS has a value of 1 if the patient is currently taking vitamins and a value of 0 if the patient is not currently taking vitamins. Notice that this variable can change for a patient from visit to visit. Run Program Appendix-2 to create the CLINICAL data set (see below).

Each patient in this data set has from one to three visits, and each visit represents one SAS observation. The variables GENDER and STATE are repeated for each visit—something that would probably not be done in practice. It would be more common to have the demographics such as date of birth, gender, or state of residence in a separate file and to merge this file with the clinical data as needed.

Notice that a PROC SORT was included, even though the data set was already in order of the dates of patient visits. The data set will need to be sorted for many of the programs that follow, so it was easier to include the sort here. A listing of the data set CLINICAL follows:

```
Listing of Data Set CLINICAL

               VISIT_
PATIENT          DATE   GENDER   STATE    HR    SBP    DBP    DX1

   001       21OCT1998     M      NJ      68    130     80    Routine Visit
   001       11NOV1998     M      NJ      66    132     78    Cold
   001       05JAN1999     M      NJ      70    140     88    Cold
   002       06MAY1999     F      NJ      78    190    100    Ear Infection
   003       04MAR2000     F      NJ      58    108     66    Cold
   003       12MAY2000     F      NJ      60    110     68    Cold
   004       30OCT1999     M      NY      88    200    110    Fracture
   004       12DEC1999     M      NY       .      .    102    Routine Visit
   004       08AUG2000     M      NY      90    180     98    Cold
   005       05MAY2000     F      NY      48    110     66    Heart Problem
   006       08AUG2000     F      NY      86    184    102    Routine Visit
   006       10OCT2000     F      NY      86      .    100    Routine Visit
   007       12DEC2000     F      NY       .      .     80    Heart Problem


PATIENT    DX2                          DX3                VITAMINS

   001                                                       No
   001                                                       No
   001     Ear Infection                                     No
   002                                                       Yes
   003                                                       Yes
   003                                                       Yes
   004     Laceration                                        No
   004                                                       Yes
   004                                                       Yes
   005     Breathing Problem                                 Yes
   006                                                       Yes
   006                                                       No
   007     Abdominal Pain      Breathing Problem             Yes
```

Notice that there are some missing values for the three cardiovascular variables (HR, SBP, and DBP).

Selecting the First or Last Visit for Each Patient

To create a separate data set containing the first or last visit for each patient, you should immediately think of the FIRST. and LAST. variables. Program 9-1 creates a data set containing the LAST visit for each patient.

Program 9-1: Creating a Data Set Containing the Last Visit for Each Patient

```
DATA LAST;
   SET CLINICAL;
   BY PATIENT;   ❶
   IF LAST.PATIENT = 1;   ❷
RUN;
```

Remember that the data set CLINICAL was previously sorted by patient number. The key here is line ❶ where you follow the SET statement with a BY statement, creating the two temporary variables FIRST.PATIENT and LAST.PATIENT. The subsetting IF statement ❷ is true only for the last visit for each patient. When the subsetting IF is true, the program continues and an implied OUTPUT is performed at the bottom of the DATA step. An alternative way of writing this statement is

```
IF LAST.PATIENT;
```

Use the statement that makes the most sense to you, not necessarily the one with the fewest keystrokes. If you also need a data set consisting of the first visit for each patient, you can create them in a single DATA step as shown in Program 9-2.

Program 9-2: Creating Two Data Sets, One for the First Visit and the Other for the Last Visit for Each Patient

```
DATA FIRST LAST;   ❶
   SET CLINICAL;
   BY PATIENT;
   IF FIRST.PATIENT = 1 THEN OUTPUT FIRST;   ❷
   IF LAST.PATIENT = 1 THEN OUTPUT LAST;   ❸
RUN;
```

Line ❶ may seem unusual to you. You can create more than one data set in a single DATA step. When you do this, it is usually necessary to specify the data set name in each of the OUTPUT statements (lines ❷ and ❸). Notice also that the second IF statement is not an ELSE IF statement. The reason is that you want patients with only one visit to be in both data sets.

A listing of the data set LAST is shown below (not all variables are included):

```
Listing of Data Set LAST

                VISIT_
PATIENT          DATE     GENDER     STATE     HR     SBP     DBP

   001        05JAN1999      M        NJ       70     140      88
   002        06MAY1999      F        NJ       78     190     100
   003        12MAY2000      F        NJ       60     110      68
   004        08AUG2000      M        NY       90     180      98
   005        05MAY2000      F        NY       48     110      66
   006        10OCT2000      F        NY       86      .      100
   007        12DEC2000      F        NY        .      .       80
```

Computing Differences between the First and Last Visits

Suppose you want to see the difference between the heart rate, systolic blood pressure, and diastolic blood pressure from the first visit to the last visit for each patient. There are several approaches to this problem, using a different combination of the tools in the first section of this book. Let's first solve this problem by using what is perhaps the most straightforward method—using retained variables. Look at Program 9-3 for this solution.

Program 9-3: Computing Differences between the First and Last Visits (Using Retained Variables)

```
DATA FIRST_LAST;
   SET CLINICAL(DROP=DX1-DX3 VITAMINS);
   BY PATIENT; ***Note: Data set already sorted;
   ***Remove patients with only one visit;
   IF FIRST.PATIENT = 1 AND LAST.PATIENT = 1 THEN DELETE;   ❶
   RETAIN FIRST_HR FIRST_SBP FIRST_DBP;   ❷

   IF FIRST.PATIENT = 1 THEN DO;   ❸
      FIRST_HR = HR;
      FIRST_SBP = SBP;
      FIRST_DBP = DBP;
   END;

   IF LAST.PATIENT = 1 THEN DO;   ❹
      DIFF_HR = HR - FIRST_HR;
      DIFF_SBP = SBP - FIRST_SBP;
      DIFF_DBP = DBP - FIRST_DBP;
      OUTPUT;   ❺
   END;

RUN;
```

```
PROC PRINT DATA=FIRST_LAST;
   TITLE "List of Data Set FIRST_LAST";
   ID PATIENT;
RUN;
```

As you can see, this program uses retained variables to "remember" the value of a variable from a previous observation. Line ❶ eliminates patients with only one visit. Remember that for such patients, both temporary variables FIRST.PATIENT and LAST.PATIENT will return a value of true. Also remember that a DELETE statement forces a return to the top of the DATA step (so no other statements below the DELETE statement will be executed).

Line ❷ requests that the three variables FIRST_HR, FIRST_SBP, and FIRST_DBP be retained. Without this statement, these variables would be replaced by missing values when the program returned to the top of the DATA step. The DO group starting in line ❸ assigns the retained variables to the values of HR, SBP, and DBP recorded at the first visit. When you get to the last visit (line ❹), you subtract the value from the first visit from the current value (which is the value at the last visit). It is important to include the OUTPUT statement ❺ here since you only want one observation per patient that includes the difference variables.

A listing of the data set FIRST_LAST is shown below:

```
List of Data Set FIRST_LAST

              V
              I
              S                           F    F
        P     I                      F    I    I         D    D
        A     T    G                 I    R    R    D    I    I
        T     _    E    S            R    S    S    I    F    F
        I     D    N    T            S    T    T    F    F    F
        E     A    D    A    S    D  T    _    _    F    _    _
        N     T    E    T    H  B  B  _   S    D    _    S    D
        T     E    R    E    R  P  P  H   B    B    H    B    B
                                    R        P    P    R    P    P

        001   05JAN1999  M   NJ   70  140   88  68  130   80   2   10    8
        003   12MAY2000  F   NJ   60  110   68  58  108   66   2    2    2
        004   08AUG2000  M   NY   90  180   98  88  200  110   2  -20  -12
        006   10OCT2000  F   NY   86    .  100  86  184  102   0    .   -2
```

Another Method of Computing Differences between the First and Last Visits

Another approach to this problem uses the LAG function, albeit in a rather unconventional way. Remember that the LAG function returns the value of its argument from the last time the function was executed. Program 9-4 executes the LAG function only when you are processing the first or the last observation for each patient. A more complete explanation follows the program.

Program 9-4: Computing Differences between the First and Last Visits (Using the LAG Function)

```
DATA FIRST_LAST;
   SET CLINICAL(DROP=DX1-DX3 VITAMINS);
   BY PATIENT; ***Note: Data set already sorted;
   ***Remove patients with only one visit;
   IF FIRST.PATIENT = 1 AND LAST.PATIENT = 1 THEN DELETE;    ❶

   IF FIRST.PATIENT = 1 OR LAST.PATIENT = 1 THEN DO;    ❷
      DIFF_HR = HR - LAG(HR);
      DIFF_SBP = SBP - LAG(SBP);
      DIFF_DBP = DBP - LAG(DBP);
   END;

   IF LAST.PATIENT = 1 THEN OUTPUT;    ❸
RUN;
```

The key to this program is line ❷. This statement says to execute the statements in the DO group only if you are processing the first or the last observation for each patient. To really understand how this works, let's follow the logic of the program for the first three patients.

• Patient 001 has three visits, so statement ❶ is not true.

• Statement ❷ is true, and the three LAG functions in the DO group are executed. The fact that the LAG values are all missing (since this is the first observation in the data set) does not cause any problems, as you will see later.

• Statement ❸ is not true, so the OUTPUT statement does not execute.

- None of the statements ❶, ❷, or ❸ is true for the second visit for patient 001.

- When you reach the third and last visit for patient 001, statement ❷ is true, and the three LAG functions are executed. The value that is returned by executing each of the LAG functions is the value of HR, SBP, and DBP the last time the LAG function was executed—the values from the first visit. So the three difference scores are computed and, since statement ❸ is now true, an observation is output to the data set FIRST_LAST.

For the compulsive programmers who are reading this book, I should point out that the three differences can be computed using the DIF function instead of the LAG function. For example, DIFF_HR could be computed as

```
DIFF_HR = DIF(HR);
```

Patient 002 has only one visit, so statement ❶ is true. The DELETE statement executes, with a return to the top of the DATA step.

What happens when you reach the first visit for patient 003? Since statement ❷ is true, the three LAG functions execute and three DIFF variables are computed. But the differences are between the last visit from patient 001 (the last time the LAG functions executed) and the first visit for patient 003! Don't worry. You are not going to output these incorrect difference scores. But it is necessary to execute the LAG functions so they will return the correct values (the values from the first visit for patient 003) when they are executed during the last visit for patient 003. When the last (second) visit for patient 003 is processed, the three difference scores are now the correct values and the OUTPUT is executed.

If you are having any problems understanding what is happening here, replace statement ❸ with a simple OUTPUT statement so you can see the values of all the variables at every visit.

The output is similar to the output from the previous program (except that the FIRST_ variables are not present).

Computing Differences between Every Visit

You may want to track a patient's heart rate and blood pressure from visit to visit. This is actually an easier problem than the one you just solved. Here you can use the LAG function in a more straightforward manner to compute the differences.

Program 9-5: Computing Differences between Every Visit (Using the LAG Function)

```
DATA DIFFERENCE;
   SET CLINICAL(DROP=DX1-DX3 VITAMINS);
   BY PATIENT;
   ***Remove patient with only one visit;
   IF FIRST.PATIENT = 1 AND LAST.PATIENT = 1 THEN DELETE;    ❶

   DIFF_HR = HR - LAG(HR);    ❷
   DIFF_SBP = SBP - LAG(SBP);
   DIFF_DBP = DBP - LAG(DBP);

   IF NOT (FIRST.PATIENT = 1) THEN OUTPUT;    ❸
RUN;
```

You see that this looks very similar to Program 9-4. You execute the LAG function for every observation and output the differences for every visit except the first (where there is no difference from a previous visit). Below is a listing of the data set DIFFERENCE:

```
List of Data Set DIFFERENCE

            VISIT_
PATIENT      DATE GENDER STATE HR SBP DBP DIFF_HR DIFF_SBP DIFF_DBP

   001    11NOV1998    M     NJ   66 132  78    -2       2        -2
   001    05JAN1999    M     NJ   70 140  88     4       8        10
   003    12MAY2000    F     NJ   60 110  68     2       2         2
   004    12DEC1999    M     NY    .   . 102     .       .        -8
   004    08AUG2000    M     NY   90 180  98     .       .        -4
   006    10OCT2000    F     NY   86   . 100     0       .        -2
```

Counting the Number of Visits for Each Patient (DATA Step Approach)

In any data set where there are a varying number of observations per subject, you may need to count the number of observations (in this case, visits) for each subject. As with most of the problems you see presented in this book, there are several solutions. Program 9-6 demonstrates a DATA step approach to this problem.

Program 9-6: Using PROC MEANS to Count the Number of Visits for Each Patient

```
DATA COUNT;
   SET CLINICAL(KEEP=PATIENT);    ❶
   BY PATIENT;
   IF FIRST.PATIENT = 1 THEN N_VISITS = 0;    ❷
   N_VISITS + 1;    ❸
   IF LAST.PATIENT = 1 THEN OUTPUT;    ❹
RUN;
```

Since you only need a single variable to count observations, the SET statement ❶ uses a KEEP= data set option for efficiency. When the first visit is being processed, statement ❷ is true, and the variable N_VISITS is set to 0. Statement ❸ increments the variable N_VISITS for each patient visit. Remember that ❸ is a SUM statement, causing the variable N_VISITS to be retained. (The fact that N_VISITS is initialized to 0 by the SUM statement has no effect since it is reset to 0 for the first visit for each patient.) You only want a single observation containing the number of visits for each patient, so you only output an observation when the last visit is reached ❹. Inspection of the listing below shows that the program is working correctly:

```
Listing of Data Set COUNT

PATIENT    N_VISITS

   001         3
   002         1
   003         2
   004         3
   005         1
   006         2
   007         1
```

If you want to add the number of visits to the original data set (CLINICAL), you can do this with a simple MERGE statement as shown in Program 9-7:

Program 9-7: Merging the Number of Visits with the Original Data Set

```
DATA NEW_CLINICAL;
   MERGE CLINICAL COUNT;
   BY PATIENT;
RUN;
```

There is no need to show a listing of this data set—it is the same as CLINICAL with the addition of the new variable N_VISITS.

Counting the Number of Visits for Each Patient (PROC FREQ)

This same problem can be solved by using PROC FREQ to do the counting. After all, isn't that what PROC FREQ was written to do? The hard part (at least for this author) is to remember the syntax to have PROC FREQ create an output data set. Program 9-8 shows how to use PROC FREQ to create an output data set of counts.

Program 9-8: Using PROC FREQ to Count the Number of Visits for Each Patient

```
PROC FREQ DATA=CLINICAL NOPRINT;   ❶
   TABLES PATIENT / OUT = COUNT(KEEP=PATIENT COUNT   ❷
                               RENAME=(COUNT = N_VISITS));
RUN;
```

Since you only want a data set and not a listing, use the NOPRINT option ❶. The OUT= option in the TABLES statement is an instruction for PROC FREQ to create an output data set. By default, PROC FREQ uses the variable name COUNT to represent the frequency. Since you want the variable to be called N_VISITS, the RENAME data set option is used ❷. In addition to the variable COUNT, PROC FREQ also outputs a variable called PERCENT (which you don't want here), so the KEEP= data set option is also used. The data set COUNT is identical to the data set produced by Program 9-6.

Which method do you prefer? If you are planning to do other calculations anyway, the DATA step approach may be more useful. If all you want is a count of the number of visits, you may prefer to use PROC FREQ. You may even want to use a third method. Continue reading to learn about additional methods.

Counting the Number of Visits for Each Patient (PROC MEANS)

You can also use PROC MEANS to count patient visits. All that is required is to have at least one numeric variable in the data set. It doesn't matter what that variable represents or if there are missing values. You can still use PROC MEANS to do the counting for you as shown in Program 9-9.

Program 9-9: Using PROC MEANS to Count the Number of Visits for Each Patient

```
PROC MEANS DATA=CLINICAL NOPRINT NWAY;    ❶
   CLASS PATIENT;    ❷
   VAR HR;    ❸
   OUTPUT OUT = COUNT(DROP=_TYPE_ N_HR    ❹
                     RENAME=(_FREQ_ = N_VISITS))
           N = N_HR;
RUN;
```

As with the PROC FREQ solution, since you don't want a listing, the NOPRINT option is used ❶. Also, since a CLASS statement ❷, rather than a BY statement, was used, the NWAY option is necessary to eliminate an extra observation corresponding to the mean of all patients. Since any numeric variable will do, HR was chosen. Also, you need to request some statistic (such as N or MEAN), even though you will throw out the result. Remember that the N= statistic represents the number of nonmissing heart rates. The variable _FREQ_ represents the number of observations in each level of the CLASS variable. As before, the RENAME= data set option renames _FREQ_ to N_VISITS. The data set COUNT is identical to the data sets produced by the previous two programs.

Counting the Number of Visits for Each Patient (PROC SQL)

PROC SQL can easily create a data set containing the number of patient visits for each patient. Program 9-10 creates a data set COUNT_VISITS that is identical to the data set from the previous programs.

Program 9-10: Using PROC SQL to Count the Number of Visits for Each Patient

```
PROC SQL;
   CREATE TABLE COUNT_VISITS AS
   SELECT PATIENT,
          COUNT(PATIENT) AS N_VISITS
   FROM CLINICAL
   GROUP BY PATIENT;    ❶
QUIT;
```

Here the COUNT function gives you the number of visits (observations) for each patient because of the GROUP BY clause ❶. Without the GROUP BY clause, the COUNT function would return the total number of observations in the data set.

Selecting All Patients with *n* Visits (DATA Step Approach)

You may have a longitudinal data set where you expect all subjects to have the same number of observations. Or, in this clinical example, you may want to select all patients with a certain number of visits. Now that you know how to count the number of visits for each patient, you can use the COUNT data set (with a minor modification) from Program 9-6, Program 9-8, Program 9-9, or Program 9-10 to accomplish this goal. For this example, suppose you want a data set of all patients in the CLINICAL data set who had exactly two visits. First, the DATA step approach as shown in Program 9-11.

Program 9-11: Using a DATA Step to Select Patients with Exactly Two Visits

```
DATA TWO;
   SET CLINICAL(KEEP=PATIENT);
   BY PATIENT;
   IF FIRST.PATIENT = 1 THEN N_VISITS = 0;
   N_VISITS + 1;
   IF LAST.PATIENT = 1 AND N_VISITS = 2 THEN OUTPUT;     ❶
RUN;


DATA TWO_VISITS;
   MERGE CLINICAL TWO(IN = IN_COUNT);     ❷
   BY PATIENT;
   IF IN_COUNT = 1;     ❸
RUN;
```

The first part of this program is identical to Program 9-6, with a change in statement ❶. Here you output an observation into the data set COUNT only when N_VISITS is equal to two. To subset the original CLINICAL data set, you can merge the two data sets (CLINICAL and TWO) using the IN= data set option. The temporary variable (IN_COUNT) is true if data set TWO is contributing to the merge, and false otherwise. So the effect of statement ❸ is to subset the

CLINICAL data set by selecting only patients who are in the data set TWO. To verify that this is working properly, you can inspect the short listing of the data set TWO_VISITS below:

```
Listing of Data Set TWO_VISITS
              V
              I
              S                                      V    N
      P       I                                      I    _
      A       T    G                                 T    V
      T       _    E    S                            A    I
      I       D    N    T                            M    S
      E       A    D    A         S    D    D   D  D I    I
      N       T    E    T    H    B    B    X   X  X N    T
      T       E    R    E    R    P    P    1   2  3 S    S

      003  04MAR2000  F   NJ   58   108   66  Cold           Yes   2
      003  12MAY2000  F   NJ   60   110   68  Cold           Yes   2
      006  08AUG2000  F   NY   86   184  102  Routine Visit  Yes   2
      006  10OCT2000  F   NY   86    .   100  Routine Visit  No    2
```

Selecting All Patients with *n* Visits (PROC FREQ Approach)

You can modify Program 9-8 to accomplish the same goal as above. Program 9-12 is just the PROC FREQ portion of the program that creates a data set (TWO) containing only patients with exactly two visits.

Program 9-12: Using PROC FREQ to Select All Patients with Exactly Two Visits

```
PROC FREQ DATA=CLINICAL NOPRINT;
   TABLES PATIENT / OUT = TWO(KEEP=PATIENT COUNT   ❷
                             RENAME=(COUNT = N_VISITS)
                             WHERE=(N_VISITS = 2));
RUN;
```

As you can see, the only change (besides the name of the output data set) is the addition of the WHERE data set option.

You can use the PROC MEANS approach in exactly the same way—it will not be shown here.

Selecting All Patients with Two Visits (Using PROC SQL)

PROC SQL can be used to create a data set containing the patient numbers for all patients with just two visits, or it can directly create a new data set, which is a subset of CLINICAL, containing all the variables for patients with exactly two visits. First, Program 9-13 demonstrates the code to create a data set of patient numbers for patients with exactly two visits.

Program 9-13: Creating a Data Set of Patient Numbers for Patients with Exactly Two Visits, One Record per Patient

```
PROC SQL;
   CREATE TABLE TWO AS
   SELECT PATIENT,
          COUNT(PATIENT) AS N_VISITS
   FROM CLINICAL
   GROUP BY PATIENT
   HAVING N_VISITS = 2;
QUIT;
```

This program is identical to Program 9-10, with the addition of the HAVING clause (and the change of the data set name in the CREATE clause).

Selecting All Patients with Two Visits (Using SQL in One Step)

If your goal is to create a new data set containing all the data from CLINICAL but containing only patients with exactly two visits, you can do this in one step (although it requires more than one pass through the data) using PROC SQL as shown in Program 9-14.

Program 9-14: Creating a Data Set of All Patient Information for Patients with Exactly Two Visits, All Records per Patient

```
PROC SQL;
   CREATE TABLE TWO_VISITS AS
   SELECT *
   FROM CLINICAL
   GROUP BY PATIENT
   HAVING COUNT(PATIENT) = 2;
QUIT;
```

The SELECT clause above uses an asterisk to select all the variables from the data set CLINICAL. The COUNT function could have been used to create a new variable (as in Program 9-13) or as part of the HAVING clause as you see here. For old-time SAS programmers, PROC SQL still seems strange, but as you can see here, it can be *very* powerful.

Using PROC SQL to Create a Macro Variable

One extremely useful feature of PROC SQL is its ability to create macro variables. In Program 9-15, you will see how Program 9-13 can be modified to create a macro variable containing the list of patient numbers with exactly two visits.

Program 9-15: Using PROC SQL to Create a Macro Variable Containing a List of Patient Numbers for Patients with Exactly Two Visits

```
PROC SQL NOPRINT;   ❶
   SELECT QUOTE(PATIENT)   ❷
   INTO :PT_LIST SEPARATED BY " "   ❸
   FROM CLINICAL
   GROUP BY PATIENT
   HAVING COUNT(PATIENT) = 2;
QUIT;
```

The key to this process is the INTO clause ❸, which instructs the SQL query to create a macro variable. Line ❶ includes the NOPRINT option since you neither want to create a data set nor to produce a listing of the resulting query. The SELECT statement ❷ uses the QUOTE function since the goal is to have each of the patient numbers in quotes (so you can use it later with an IN comparison operator). Again, thinking ahead, an IN comparison operator, when used with a character variable, can be a list of quoted values separated by either spaces or commas. We chose spaces. (If you prefer commas, simply modify line ❸ by placing a comma between the double quotes, instead of a space.) The remainder of the program has been explained previously.

The macro variable PT_LIST is the text string

```
"003" "006" "007"
```

An example of how this macro variable could be used is shown in Program 9-16.

Program 9-16: Demonstrating How to Use the Previously Generated Macro Variable

```
PROC PRINT DATA=CLINICAL;
   WHERE PATIENT IN (&PT_LIST);
   TITLE "Subset of Patients with Exactly Two Visits";
RUN;
```

Computing Summary Statistics for Each Patient (Using PROC MEANS)

Since you have multiple visits per patient in the CLINICAL data set, you may want to compute patient means. Program 9-17 shows how to do this using PROC MEANS.

Program 9-17: Computing Summary Statistics for Each Patient (Using PROC MEANS)

```
PROC MEANS DATA=CLINICAL NOPRINT NWAY;    ❶
   CLASS PATIENT;
   VAR HR SBP DBP;
   OUTPUT OUT  = PT_MEANS(DROP=_TYPE_    ❷
                       RENAME=(_FREQ_ = N_VISITS))
          N    = N_HR N_SBP N_DBP    ❸
          MEAN = MEAN_HR MEAN_SBP MEAN_DBP;    ❹
RUN;

PROC PRINT DATA=PT_MEANS;
   TITLE "Listing of Data Set PT_MEANS";
   ID PATIENT;
RUN;
```

Don't forget to include the two options NOPRINT and NWAY ❶ when you use PROC MEANS to produce a summary data set. (If you use a BY statement instead of a CLASS statement, you can omit the NWAY option.) The output data set (PT_MEANS) is created by the OUTPUT statement ❷. In this example, you are requesting the number of nonmissing values ❸ and the mean values ❹ for the three variables listed in the VAR statement. A listing of the new PT_MEANS data set is shown next:

```
Listing of Data Set PT_MEANS

PATIENT  N_VISITS  N_HR  N_SBP  N_DBP  MEAN_HR  MEAN_SBP  MEAN_DBP
  001        3       3     3      3       68       134      82.000
  002        1       1     1      1       78       190     100.000
  003        2       2     2      2       59       109      67.000
  004        3       2     2      3       89       190     103.333
  005        1       1     1      1       48       110      66.000
  006        2       2     1      2       86       184     101.000
  007        1       0     0      1        .         .      80.000
```

Computing Summary Statistics for Each Patient (Using PROC SQL)

How about using PROC SQL to accomplish the same goal as Program 9-17? Program 9-18 demonstrates how to do this.

Program 9-18: Using PROC SQL to Compute Summary Statistics for Each Patient

```
PROC SQL;
   CREATE TABLE PT_MEANS AS
   SELECT PATIENT,
          COUNT(HR) AS N_HR,
          COUNT(SBP) AS N_SBP,
          COUNT(DBP) AS N_DBP,
          COUNT(PATIENT) AS N_VISITS,
          AVG(HR) AS MEAN_HR,
          AVG(SBP) AS MEAN_SBP,
          AVG(DBP) AS MEAN_DBP
   FROM CLINICAL
   GROUP BY PATIENT;
QUIT;
```

Here you see the two SQL functions COUNT and AVG used to produce the desired statistics. Again, it is critical to include the GROUP BY clause so that the statistics are computed for each value of the grouping variable (PATIENT). A listing of the data set PT_MEANS follows:

```
Listing of Data Set PT_MEANS

Obs   PATIENT   N_HR   N_SBP   N_DBP   N_VISITS   MEAN_HR   MEAN_SBP   MEAN_DBP

 1      001       3      3       3         3         68        134       82.000
 2      002       1      1       1         1         78        190      100.000
 3      003       2      2       2         2         59        109       67.000
 4      004       2      2       3         3         89        190      103.333
 5      005       1      1       1         1         48        110       66.000
 6      006       2      1       2         2         86        184      101.000
 7      007       0      0       1         1         .          .        80.000
```

Adding a Value from the First Visit to Each Subsequent Visit

It is not that uncommon for people (usually unfamiliar with data processing) to collect longitudinal data with constant values (such as DOB or GENDER) entered only on the first observation. For example, run Program Appendix-3 to create a data set (CLIN_FIRST) in which the variables GENDER and STATE are entered only for the first visit:

```
Listing of Data Set CLIN_FIRST

                 V
                 I
                 S                                                        V
     P           I                                                       I
     A         T G                                                       T
     T         _ E S                                                     A
     I         D N T                                                     M
O    E         A D A   S  D   D          D                   D          I
b    N         T E T H B   B  X          X                   X          N
s    T         E R E R  P  P  1          2                   3          S

 1  001 21OCT1998 M NJ 68 130  80 Routine Visit                         No
 2  001 11NOV1998      66 132  78 Cold                                  No
 3  001 05JAN1999      70 140  88 Cold          Ear Infection           No
 4  002 06MAY1999 F NJ 78 190 100 Ear Infection                         Yes
 5  003 04MAR2000 F NJ 58 108  66 Cold                                  Yes
 6  003 12MAY2000      60 110  68 Cold                                  Yes
 7  004 30OCT1999 M NY 88 200 110 Fracture      Laceration              No
 8  004 12DEC1999       .   . 102 Routine Visit                         Yes
 9  004 08AUG2000      90 180  98 Cold                                  Yes
10  005 05MAY2000 F NY 48 110  66 Heart Problem Breathing Problem       Yes
11  006 08AUG2000 F NY 86 184 102 Routine Visit                         Yes
12  006 10OCT2000      86   . 100 Routine Visit                         No
13  007 12DEC2000 F NY  .   .  80 Heart Problem Abdominal Pain   Breathing Problem Yes
```

One way to add GENDER and STATE to each observation is to use retained variables as shown in Program 9-19.

Program 9-19: Adding GENDER and STATE to Each Visit (After the First)

```
DATA CLIN_EVERY;
   RETAIN FIRST_GENDER FIRST_STATE;
   SET CLIN_FIRST;
   BY PATIENT;

   IF FIRST.PATIENT = 1 THEN DO;     ❶
      FIRST_GENDER = GENDER;
      FIRST_STATE  = STATE;
   END;

ELSE DO;
      GENDER = FIRST_GENDER;
      STATE  = FIRST_STATE;
   END;

   DROP FIRST_:;     ❷
RUN;
```

When you are processing the first visit for each patient, FIRST.PATIENT returns a value of true, and the DO GROUP ❶ executes. For every other visit, the ELSE DO statements execute, and GENDER and STATE are set to the retained values. The colon notation ❷ is a shortcut way of listing all variables that begin with the characters FIRST_. That is, the colon acts as a wild card.

The listing of the data set CLIN_EVERY verifies that Program 9-19 works as designed.

```
Listing of Data Set CLIN_EVERY

                 V
                 I
                 S                                                       V
        P        I                                                       I
        A        T G                                                     T
        T        _ E S                                                   A
        I        D N T                                                   M
  O     E        A D A      S   D   D          D                D        I
  b     N        T E T   H  B   B   X          X                X        N
  s     T        E R E   R  P   P   1          2                3        S
   1 001 21OCT1998 M NJ 68 130  80 Routine Visit                         No
   2 001 11NOV1998 M NJ 66 132  78 Cold                                  No
   3 001 05JAN1999 M NJ 70 140  88 Cold          Ear Infection           No
   4 002 06MAY1999 F NJ 78 190 100 Ear Infection                        Yes
   5 003 04MAR2000 F NJ 58 108  66 Cold                                 Yes
   6 003 12MAY2000 F NJ 60 110  68 Cold                                 Yes
   7 004 30OCT1999 M NY 88 200 110 Fracture      Laceration             No
   8 004 12DEC1999 M NY  .   . 102 Routine Visit                       Yes
   9 004 08AUG2000 M NY 90 180  98 Cold                                 Yes
  10 005 05MAY2000 F NY 48 110  66 Heart Problem Breathing Problem      Yes
  11 006 08AUG2000 F NY 86 184 102 Routine Visit                       Yes
  12 006 10OCT2000 F NY 86   . 100 Routine Visit                        No
  13 007 12DEC2000 F NY  .   .  80 Heart Problem Abdominal Pain  Breathing Problem Yes
```

Looking Ahead: Making a Decision about the Current Observation Based on Information in the Next Observation

You have seen that SAS has several powerful tools for looking back, allowing you to make decisions about the current observation based on information from previous observations. Retained variables and the LAG functions come to mind. However, suppose you want to make a decision based on information from an observation that comes after the one you are currently processing.

Did you know that you can have more than one SET statement with the same data set name in a single DATA step? Well, you can. You can use multiple SET statements in combination with the FIRSTOBS= data set option to "look ahead."

Program 9-20 is based on a program that was written to investigate the patient and doctor characteristics that might be related to a treatment failure for ear infections. First, run Program 9-20 to create a small test data set called DOC. This data set contains patients with a diagnosis of ear infection, the date of their visit (VISIT), and the initials of the doctor who treated them.

Program 9-20: Creating a Test Data Set of Doctor Visits

```
DATA DOC;
    INPUT @1   PATIENT    $3.
          @5   VISIT      MMDDYY10.
          @16 DOCTOR      $3.;
    FORMAT VISIT MMDDYY10.;
DATALINES;
001 10/21/1998 ABC
001 10/29/1998 XYZ
001 12/12/1998 QED
002 01/01/1998 ABC
003 02/13/1998 QED
003 04/15/1998 MAD
005 05/06/1998 XYZ
005 05/08/1998 QED
RUN;
```

The goal is to identify any patient who returns within 30 days and to define this as a treatment failure. Look at the first visit in the data listed in the program. Notice that patient 001 returns in eight days. This treatment failure is attributed to doctor ABC. So it would be convenient to be able to look ahead to the next patient visit to see if the same patient returned within 30 days for treatment. If you execute a SET statement twice, once with no data set options and the second time with FIRSTOBS=2, you can have the values from the current observation and the next observation in the same program data vector (the place where values of variables are stored during each iteration of the DATA step). Obviously, you will need to rename some of the variables or the values of one would be overwritten by the other. Examine Program 9-21.

Program 9-21: Looking Ahead Using Multiple SET Statements

```
PROC SORT DATA=DOC;
   BY PATIENT VISIT;
RUN;

DATA FAILURES;
   SET DOC;     ❶
   BY PATIENT;   ❷
   SET DOC (FIRSTOBS = 2   ❸
            KEEP = VISIT
            RENAME = (VISIT = NEXT_VISIT));
   IF LAST.PATIENT = 0 AND (NEXT_VISIT - VISIT) LT 30 THEN OUTPUT;   ❹
   KEEP PATIENT VISIT NEXT_VISIT DOCTOR;
RUN;
```

The first SET statement ❶ brings in an observation from the data set DOC, starting with the first. The BY statement ❷ creates the two temporary variables FIRST.PATIENT and LAST.PATIENT. Note that these two temporary variables are associated with the observations being read with the first SET statement. The second SET statement ❸ includes the FIRSTOBS=2 option so that it starts bringing in observations from the data set DOC, starting with the second observation. The variable name VISIT is changed to NEXT_VISIT using the RENAME= option. Statement ❹ outputs an observation to the data set FAILURES if this is not the last visit for this patient and the value of NEXT_VISIT is within 30 days of VISIT. (There is no way to determine if the last visit for a patient is a failure, so no outputting is done when the last visit is being processed.)

The resulting data set FAILURES is listed below:

```
Listing of Data Set FAILURES

PATIENT         VISIT    DOCTOR    NEXT_VISIT

  001       10/21/1998    ABC      10/29/1998
  005       05/06/1998    XYZ      05/08/1998
```

Using Flags to Ascertain Vitamin Use

Information on the use of vitamins is entered for each visit (observation) in the clinical database. The same patient may be taking vitamins during some visits and not at others. You might want to determine if a patient *ever* used vitamins. As with many SAS solutions, there are several different approaches to this problem. One straightforward approach is to use a retained variable to "remember" if a particular patient ever used vitamins. Look at Program 9-22.

Program 9-22: Using a Flag to Remember Information from Previous Observations

```
DATA VITAMIN_EVER;
   SET CLINICAL(KEEP = PATIENT VITAMINS);
   BY PATIENT;
   RETAIN FLAG;         ❶
   IF FIRST.PATIENT = 1 THEN FLAG = 0;    ❷
   IF VITAMINS = '1' THEN FLAG = 1;    ❸
   IF LAST.PATIENT = 1 THEN OUTPUT;    ❹
   DROP VITAMINS;
RUN;
```

Each time you encounter a new patient, the flag is reset to 0 ❷. If the value of the variable VITAMINS is equal to "1," the flag is "turned on" (set equal to 1). Since FLAG is retained, it will remain equal to 1 until it is reset back to 0 when a new patient is encountered. So when the OUTPUT occurs ❹, the value of FLAG will be 1 for any patient who had one or more visits where vitamins were used. The listing below confirms that this program works as designed:

```
Listing of Data Set VITAMIN_EVER

PATIENT    FLAG

  001        0
  002        1
  003        1
  004        1
  005        1
  006        1
  007        1
```

Using PROC FREQ to Ascertain Vitamin Use

Another approach to this problem is to first create an output data set using PROC FREQ and then write a small DATA step to create a variable that indicates if vitamins were ever used by each patient. This is shown in Program 9-23.

Program 9-23: Using PROC FREQ to Ascertain Vitamin Use

```
PROC FREQ DATA=CLINICAL NOPRINT;
    TABLES PATIENT*VITAMINS / OUT=SUMMARY(DROP = PERCENT);    ❶
RUN;

DATA VITAMIN_EVER;
    SET SUMMARY;
    BY PATIENT;
    IF VITAMINS = '1' AND COUNT GT 0 THEN USE_VITAMINS = 1;    ❷
    ELSE USE_VITAMINS = 0;
    IF LAST.PATIENT = 1 THEN OUTPUT;    ❸
    KEEP PATIENT USE_VITAMINS;
RUN;
```

Since VITAMINS is a character variable, you use PROC FREQ to count the number of 1's and 0's (character values) ❶. The output data set from PROC FREQ (SUMMARY) will contain either one or two observations for each patient—one if the patient had all 1's or all 0's, and two if the patient had at least one value of "1" and one value of "0." The data set SUMMARY is shown below:

```
Listing of Data Set SUMMARY

Obs     PATIENT    VITAMINS    COUNT

1       001        No          3
2       002        Yes         1
3       003        Yes         2
4       004        No          1
5       004        Yes         2
6       005        Yes         1
7       006        No          1
8       006        Yes         1
9       007        Yes         1
```

Therefore, it is necessary to make sure the COUNT variable (the variable created by PROC FREQ) is tested only when the value of VITAMINS is equal to "1" (formatted as Yes). A listing of the data set VITAMIN_EVER follows:

```
Listing of Data Set VITAMIN_EVER

                    USE_
Obs     PATIENT    VITAMINS

1         001         0
2         002         1
3         003         1
4         004         1
5         005         1
6         006         1
7         007         1
```

Counting the Number of Routine Visits for Each Patient

A diagnosis code of "1" represents a routine visit. Using similar logic to Program 9-22, you can count the number of routine visits for each patient. Remember that a SUM statement causes a variable to be retained and to be initialized at zero.

Program 9-24: Using a SUM Statement and FIRST. and LAST. Logic to Count the Number of Routine Visits for Each Patient

```
DATA ROUTINE;
   SET CLINICAL(KEEP = PATIENT DX1-DX3);
   BY PATIENT;
   IF FIRST.PATIENT = 1 THEN N_ROUTINE = 0;   ❶
   IF DX1= '1' OR DX2 = '1' OR DX3 = '1' THEN N_ROUTINE + 1;   ❷
   IF LAST.PATIENT = 1 THEN OUTPUT;   ❸
   KEEP PATIENT N_ROUTINE;
RUN;
```

The variable N_ROUTINE is set to 0 for each new patient ❶. The SUM statement ❷ increments the count every time a patient comes in for a routine visit. A single observation is written out to the ROUTINE data set after the last visit for each patient has been processed ❸.

A listing of ROUTINE is shown next:

```
Listing of Data Set ROUTINE

PATIENT    N_ROUTINE

  001          1
  002          0
  003          0
  004          1
  005          0
  006          2
  007          0
```

As you can see, the tools developed earlier can be extremely useful when dealing with data such as the clinical data set. Many of the problems presented in this chapter were solved using a variety of techniques. The method you choose may depend on what you are more comfortable with: DATA step programming, procedures that produce output data sets, PROC SQL, etc. When processing very large data sets, you may need to test several methods with sample data if efficiency is an issue.

10 Study Two: Operations on Daily Weather Data and Ozone Levels

Introduction

Data for this chapter consists of daily ozone levels, daily pollen and spore counts, and maximum daily temperature from May 1, 1995, to July 31, 1995. The techniques that will be demonstrated include computing weekly and moving averages. These techniques are useful to show trends in data values over time when there are large day-to-day fluctuations in the values. Economists use moving averages to look at stock prices or other values when they want to examine long-term trends.

The OZONE Data Set

Run Program Appendix-4 to create the OZONE data set. The variables are the date the observation was made; the spore count, pollen count, and ozone level on that date; and the maximum temperature recorded for that date. A listing of the first 10 observations from this data set is shown below:

```
Listing of Data Set OZONE
First 10 Observations

Obs          DATE     SPORES    POLLEN    OZONE    MAX_TEMP

  1    05/01/1995       876      2261      36.3       62
  2    05/02/1995      1377      2711      32.0       53
  3    05/03/1995       800      2142      43.7       75
  4    05/04/1995      1421      4029      42.5       71
  5    05/05/1995      1599      6284      33.0       64
  6    05/06/1995      1322      4228      53.6       70
  7    05/07/1995      1322      4109      49.1       71
  8    05/08/1995      1322      4109      39.8       70
  9    05/09/1995       998      1915      43.4       72
 10    05/10/1995      1134      2450      45.3       56
```

Computing Weekly Averages

Because several of the variables in this data set fluctuate considerably from day-to-day, you might be able to detect long-term trends by examining weekly averages, rather than the daily values. Program 10-1 shows how you can accomplish this, using a DATA step together with PROC MEANS.

Program 10-1: Using PROC MEANS and the INTCK Function to Compute Weekly Averages

```
DATA WEEK_NUM;
   SET OZONE;
   WEEK_NUMBER = INTCK('WEEK','01MAY1995'D,DATE) + 1;   ❶
RUN;


PROC MEANS DATA=WEEK_NUM NOPRINT NWAY;
   CLASS WEEK_NUMBER;
   VAR SPORES POLLEN OZONE MAX_TEMP;
   OUTPUT OUT=WEEKLY_MEANS
          MEAN=M_SPORES M_POLLEN M_OZONE M_MAX_TEMP;
RUN;
```

The key to Program 10-1 is line ❶ of the DATA step. Starting from the first day of May, 1995 (which happens to be a Monday), you create a variable called WEEK_NUMBER, which is equal to the number of Sundays that have passed since May 1, 1995.

The INTCK function is difficult to understand (and hard to pronounce). It computes the number of intervals between two given dates. More specifically, it returns the number of "boundaries" that have been crossed between the two dates. For example, if the interval is YEAR, and the first date is December 31, 2000, and the second date is January 1, 2001, the INTCK function will return a 1 (you cross a year boundary when going from the first date to the second). If the first date is January 1, 2000, and the second date is December 31, 2000, the INTCK function will return a 0, because no year boundaries have been crossed.

The function takes the form

```
INTCK('interval',first_date,second_date)
```

where interval can take on values such as QTR, WEEK, TENDAY, MONTH, or YEAR (see SAS OnlineDoc for a complete list). If the interval is WEEK, the number of intervals is determined by the number of Sundays between the two dates. For example, the statement

```
INTERVAL = INTCK('WEEK','01MAY1995'D,DATE);
```

will return the number of Sundays that have elapsed between May 1, 1995, and DATE. In Program 10-1, a 1 is added to the value so that WEEK_NUMBER starts from 1 rather than from 0. Below is a listing of the first 15 observations in the data set WEEK_NUM:

```
Listing of Data Set WEEK_NUM
First 15 Observations


                                                                    WEEK_
 Obs          DATE      SPORES    POLLEN     OZONE    MAX_TEMP      NUMBER
   1      05/01/1995      876      2261      36.3        62           1
   2      05/02/1995     1377      2711      32.0        53           1
   3      05/03/1995      800      2142      43.7        75           1
   4      05/04/1995     1421      4029      42.5        71           1
   5      05/05/1995     1599      6284      33.0        64           1
   6      05/06/1995     1322      4228      53.6        70           1
   7      05/07/1995     1322      4109      49.1        71           2
   8      05/08/1995     1322      4109      39.8        70           2
   9      05/09/1995      998      1915      43.4        72           2
  10      05/10/1995     1134      2450      45.3        56           2
  11      05/11/1995      589      1619      26.4        59           2
  12      05/12/1995     1545       788      26.2        63           2
  13      05/13/1995     2397      2642      51.1        75           2
  14      05/14/1995     2397      2642      33.4        66           3
  15      05/15/1995     2397      2642      31.8        76           3
```

Since May 1, 1995, is a Monday, there are only six values in the first group (WEEK_NUMBER = 1). If you wanted all the groups to contain exactly seven values, you could write a short DATA step to throw out values until the first Sunday was processed.

The PROC MEANS part of the program computes means for each week (different value of WEEK_NUMBER). You can now use the new data set (WEEKLY_MEANS) to look at weekly trends. For example, run Program 10-2 to see the plot showing the weekly pollen levels by WEEK_NUMBER.

Program 10-2: Plotting Weekly Pollen Means

```
SYMBOL VALUE=DOT INTERPOL=JOIN;
PROC GPLOT DATA=WEEKLY_MEANS;
   TITLE "Mean Pollen Levels by Week";
   PLOT M_POLLEN * WEEK_NUMBER;
RUN;
QUIT;
```

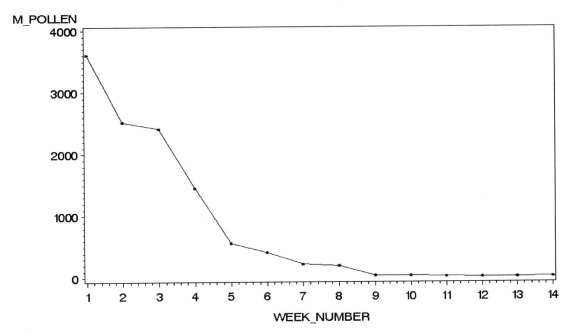

Using the MOD Function to Group Data Values

You may want to group a series of data values to compute group means when you don't have a date value. Run Program 10-3 to create a small test data set of scores.

Program 10-3: Creating a Test Data Set to Demonstrate Another Way to Group Values

```
DATA TEST;
   INPUT X @@;
DATALINES;
1 6 3 9 3 9 7 1 9 3 8 4 10 3 9 3
;
```

Suppose you want to compute the mean of every four values. Remember that the MOD function

```
MOD(A,B)
```

returns the remainder when you divide A by B. For example, MOD (5,4) is equal to 1; so is MOD (9,4) and MOD (13,4). Let's see how you can use the MOD function to create groups of four from the TEST data set.

Program 10-4: Using the MOD Function to Group Data Values

```
DATA GROUPING;
   SET TEST;
   GROUP + (MOD(_N_ ,4) EQ 1);
RUN;
```

Program 10-4 uses the internal variable _N_, which counts iterations of the DATA step and the MOD function to create a GROUP variable. The MOD function takes two arguments: The value that the MOD function returns is the remainder when the first argument is divided by the second argument. For example, MOD (5,4) (this is read as 5 mod 4) is equal to 1 (the remainder when 5 is divided by 4). MOD (6,4) returns a 2 and MOD (7,4) returns a 3, and so forth. Therefore, when _N_ has a value of 1, 5, 9, etc. (that is, every 4), the MOD function returns a 1, the logical expression (MOD(_N_ ,4) EQ 1) is true (equal to 1), and GROUP is incremented. Look at the listing of the data set GROUPING below:

```
Listing of Data Set GROUPING

Obs     X     GROUP

  1     1       1
  2     6       1
  3     3       1
  4     9       1
  5     3       2
  6     9       2
  7     7       2
  8     1       2
  9     9       3
 10     3       3
 11     8       3
 12     4       3
 13    10       4
 14     3       4
 15     9       4
 16     3       4
```

You can now use GROUP as a CLASS or BY variable with PROC MEANS to compute means of groups of size four.

Computing a Moving Average for a Single Variable

Rather than compute a mean for each week of data, you can compute what is called a moving average. Moving averages are often used with economic data that have large fluctuations. A moving average can be computed with any number of data points in each average. For example, if you have a series of values like this

```
1 3 9 2 10
```

a moving average, using an interval of two, would be the mean of 1 and 3; 3 and 9; 9 and 2; 2 and 10, yielding 2, 6, 5.5, and 6. A simple program to look at ozone levels with a moving average, using an interval of 5 days, is shown in Program 10-5.

Program 10-5: Computing a Moving Average for Ozone Levels (Using Groups of 5)

```
DATA MOVING;
   SET OZONE(KEEP=DATE OZONE);   ❶
   OZONE_LAG24 = LAG(OZONE);
   OZONE_LAG48 = LAG2(OZONE);
   OZONE_LAG72 = LAG3(OZONE);
   OZONE_LAG96 = LAG4(OZONE);
   IF _N_ GE 5 THEN OZONE_AVE = MEAN(OF OZONE OZONE_:);   ❷
RUN;

SYMBOL1 VALUE = POINT INTERPOL=JOIN L=1 COLOR=BLACK;
SYMBOL2 VALUE = POINT INTERPOL=JOIN L=3 COLOR=BLACK;
PROC GPLOT DATA=MOVING;
   TITLE "Raw and Moving Average Data for Ozone in the Month of May";
   WHERE DATE BETWEEN '01MAY1995'D AND '31MAY1995'D;
   PLOT OZONE*DATE OZONE_AVE*DATE / OVERLAY;
RUN;
QUIT;
```

The data set MOVING is created by averaging the current ozone level with the levels from the previous four days. The family of LAG*n* functions provides the values from the previous observations (technically, from the previous executions of the LAG function). Calculating the ozone moving average begins with the fifth observation since you want to average the current observation and the previous four. Notice the use of the colon notation in line ❷. OZONE_: means to include all variables starting with the characters OZONE_.

An alternative approach is to output the first value, then the average of the first two, the first three, etc., until you reach observation number five. With this approach, the first four data values are not averages of five values.

To see the effect of a moving average, the statements to plot the raw and averaged values for the month of May were included. The output below resulted from running these statements:

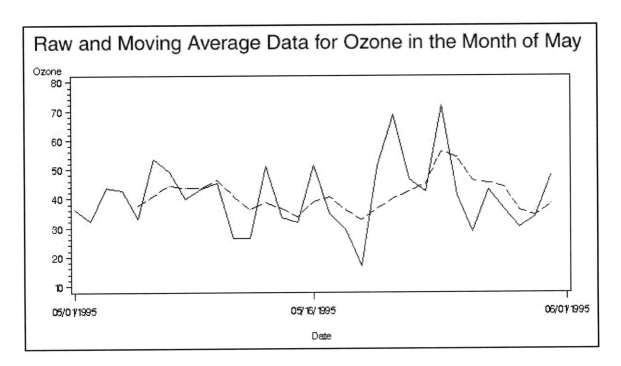

Raw and Moving Average Data for Ozone in the Month of May

Note: The dotted line represents the moving average.

Notice how the moving average smoothes out the curve compared to the raw values.

In this chapter, you have seen two useful methods for computing averages to see long-term trends in data values that are highly variable. The simpler method is to group the data values and compute the average of each group. Using a moving average is slightly more complicated but usually does a better job in detecting trends in the data. You will find a useful macro for computing moving averages in Chapter 12.

11 Study Three: Producing Summary Reports on a Library Data Set

Introduction

This chapter uses a small data set that represents books borrowed from two different libraries. Each observation in the LIBRARY data set represents a single book, and each borrower can check out one or more books at each visit. What makes this data set interesting is that it can be broken down in many ways. For example, the unit of analysis could be patron visits, LC (Library of Congress) categories, age groups, and so forth. You may want to know the average number of books taken out by each patron, overall, and for each library separately. Or, you may want to see the total number of books in each of the LC categories, broken down by age group.

To get started run Program Appendix-5 to create the LIBRARY data. A listing of the first 15 observations from this data set is shown below:

```
Listing of Data Set LIBRARY
First 15 Observations

                                                    AGE_
Obs  ID     LIBRARY      DATE      LC      CATEGORY         GROUP  DUE_DATE DAY

  1 Y0123 CLINTON     21OCT2000 H410.B5  Social Sciences Youth 04NOV2000 Sat.
  2 Y0123 CLINTON     21OCT2000 H415.A7  Social Sciences Youth 04NOV2000 Sat.
  3 A1234 FLEMINGTON  21OCT2000 Q550.B10 Science         Adult 04NOV2000 Sat.
```

```
 4 A1234 FLEMINGTON 21OCT2000 Q550.C8  Science      Adult 04NOV2000 Sat.
 5 A1234 FLEMINGTON 21OCT2000 M410.C12 Music        Adult 04NOV2000 Sat.
 6 A2121 CLINTON    21OCT2000 PA317.A9 Literature   Adult 04NOV2000 Sat.
 7 Y8888 FLEMINGTON 21OCT2000 E110.A1  History      Youth 04NOV2000 Sat.
 8 Y8888 FLEMINGTON 21OCT2000 F441.B9  History      Youth 04NOV2000 Sat.
 9 A7654 FLEMINGTON 21OCT2000 ML440.B5 Music        Adult 04NOV2000 Sat.
10 A8765 CLINTON    21OCT2000 L550.V5  Education     Adult 04NOV2000 Sat.
11 A8765 CLINTON    21OCT2000 L550.D3  Education     Adult 04NOV2000 Sat.
12 A8765 CLINTON    21OCT2000 L550.E3  Education     Adult 04NOV2000 Sat.
13 A8765 CLINTON    21OCT2000 L551.A6  Education     Adult 04NOV2000 Sat.
14 Y6565 FLEMINGTON 23OCT2000 Q220.B7  Science      Youth 06NOV2000 Mon.
15 Y6565 FLEMINGTON 23OCT2000 Q220.C7  Science      Youth 06NOV2000 Mon.
```

As you can see, the variables for each visit include a patron ID, a library location, the transaction date, an LC number for each book borrowed, an LC category computed from the LC number (see details in the Appendix), an age group designation (Adult or Youth), a due date, and the day of the week (the last two computed from the transaction date).

Computing the Number of Books per Patron Visit and by Library

Our first task will be to generate a frequency distribution for the number of books checked out of the library by each patron. This will be done overall and by library. Both PROC MEANS and PROC FREQ come to mind as ways of solving this problem. Program 11-1 uses a PROC MEANS solution.

Program 11-1: Using PROC MEANS to Compute Counts and Averages for Books Borrowed

```
PROC MEANS DATA=LIBRARY NOPRINT CHARTYPE;   ❶
   CLASS ID DATE LIBRARY;   ❷
   TYPES ID*DATE ID*DATE*LIBRARY;   ❸
   VAR DATE;
   OUTPUT OUT=BOOKS(DROP=_FREQ_) N = N_OF_BOOKS;
RUN;
```

Since you want to see the number of books taken out by each patron on a given date, you can use ID and DATE as CLASS variables in PROC MEANS. But since you also want to see a breakdown of the borrowing frequencies for each of the libraries separately, you can include LIBRARY in the CLASS list ❷. Realizing that there will be eight values of the _TYPE_ variable, you can select which counts you want to keep, using a TYPES statement ❸. The CHARTYPE option ❶ creates a character _TYPE_ variable instead of the usual binary (numeric) value. The only trick is to figure out which values of _TYPE_ correspond to the book counts that you want.

Since the variables in the CLASS statement are ID, DATE, and LIBRARY, you can see that _TYPE_ "110" corresponds to the number of books borrowed by each patron on a given date, and "111" corresponds to this same number, broken down by LIBRARY. Let's look at the output data set (BOOKS) to help make this rather complicated idea a bit clearer. Here is a partial listing:

```
Partial Listing of Data Set BOOKS


                                                             N_OF_
Obs      ID          DATE      LIBRARY        _TYPE_        BOOKS

  1     A1010      23OCT2000                    110            4
  2     A1022      23OCT2000                    110            3
  3     A1234      21OCT2000                    110            3
  4     A1234      28OCT2000                    110            3
  5     A1747      30OCT2000                    110            1
  6     A2121      21OCT2000                    110            1
  7     A2121      01NOV2000                    110            2
  8     A2121      06NOV2000                    110            2
  9     A2345      24OCT2000                    110            2
                              .
                              .
                              .

 32     A1010      23OCT2000   FLEMINGTON       111            4
 33     A1022      23OCT2000   CLINTON          111            3
 34     A1234      21OCT2000   FLEMINGTON       111            3
 35     A1234      28OCT2000   CLINTON          111            3
                              .
                              .
                              .
```

Notice that when the value of _TYPE_ is "110" (remember this is a character string because of the CHARTYPE procedure option), the observations represent the number of books checked out by each patron on a given date, regardless of which library was visited. When _TYPE_ is equal to "111," the observations represent the number of books taken out by each patron at a specific library.

Now, if you want to see statistics on the number of books taken out by each patron, on a given date, either overall or by library, you have the values you need. For example, to compute the mean and standard deviation on the number of books borrowed, independent of library, you can run PROC MEANS again, with the WHERE statement

```
WHERE _TYPE_ = "110";
```

To see these statistics broken down by LIBRARY, you can substitute the statement

```
WHERE _TYPE_ = "111";
```

Program 11-2 produces a chart showing the frequencies of books taken out by each patron on a given date in each of the libraries.

Program 11-2: Using PROC CHART to Display Book Frequencies by Library

```
PROC CHART DATA = BOOKS;
   WHERE _TYPE_ = "111";
   TITLE "Book Frequencies by Library";
   VBAR N_OF_BOOKS / GROUP = LIBRARY MIDPOINTS = 0 TO 5 BY 1;
RUN;
```

Output from this procedure is shown below:

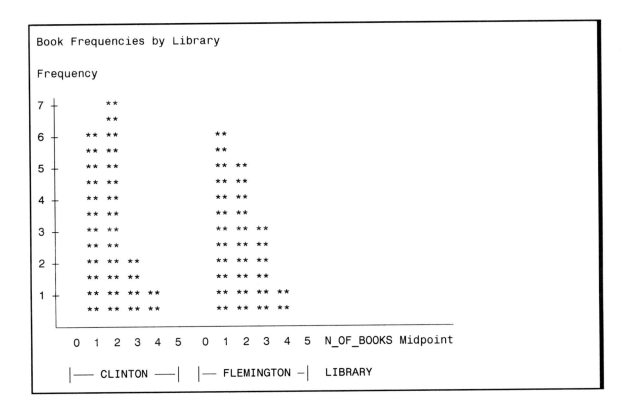

```
Book Frequencies by Library

Frequency

  7 +          **
                **
  6 +    ** **              **
         ** **              **
  5 +    ** **              ** **
         ** **              ** **
  4 +    ** **              ** **
         ** **              ** **
  3 +    ** **              ** ** **
         ** **              ** ** **
  2 +    ** ** **           ** ** **
         ** ** **           ** ** **
  1 +    ** ** ** **        ** ** ** **
         ** ** ** **        ** ** ** **

        0 1 2 3 4 5   0 1 2 3 4 5   N_OF_BOOKS Midpoint

        |— CLINTON —|   |— FLEMINGTON —|   LIBRARY
```

Computing the Number of Patrons by Day of Week and Library

Suppose you want to see how the number of books taken out by patrons changes by day of the week and library. You can rerun Program 11-1 and change the CLASS and TYPES statements. You can then use the output data set to inspect the distribution. Program 11-3 computes the book frequencies by day of the week and library.

Program 11-3: Computing the Book Frequency by Day of the Week and Library

```
PROC MEANS DATA=LIBRARY NOPRINT NWAY;
   CLASS ID DAY LIBRARY;
   VAR DATE;
   OUTPUT OUT=BOOKS_BY_DAY(DROP = _TYPE_ _FREQ_) N = N_OF_BOOKS;
RUN;


PROC CHART DATA = BOOKS_BY_DAY;
   TITLE "Book Frequencies by Day of the Week and Library";
   VBAR DAY / SUMVAR = N_OF_BOOKS
              TYPE = MEAN
              GROUP = LIBRARY
              DISCRETE;
RUN;
```

Since you only want the number of books for each combination of ID, DAY, and LIBRARY, you can use the NWAY option of PROC MEANS. This option restricts the statistics in the output data set to the highest value of the _TYPE_ variable (7, in this case, or "111" if you used the CHARTYPE procedure option). Another way of saying this is that the output data set will contain statistics only for each combination of the CLASS variables. A DROP data set option on the output data set is included in the procedure to omit the two variables, _TYPE_ and _FREQ_. The variable DAY is numeric (with an appropriate format), so the DISCRETE option on the VBAR statement is necessary to prevent PROC CHART from grouping the values on the x-axis rather than using the actual DAY values. The resulting chart is shown next:

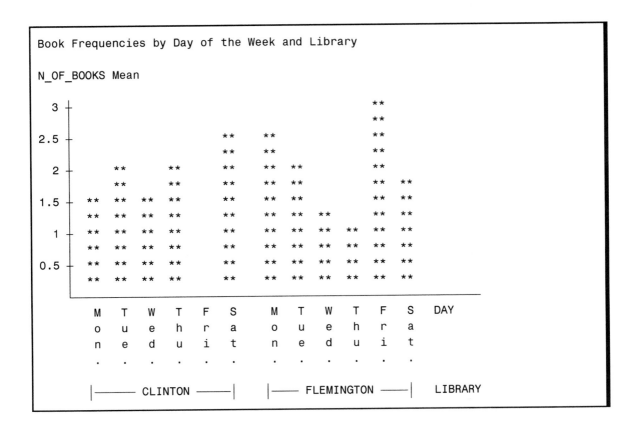

Generating a Table of LC Categories by Age Group and Overall

The final example in this chapter uses PROC TABULATE to compute how many books are borrowed in each LC category, broken down by age group and overall.

Program 11-4: Using PROC TABULATE to Display Book Frequencies by LC Category, Age Group, and Overall

```
PROC TABULATE DATA=LIBRARY;
   TITLE "Frequencies of Books by LC Category and Age Group";
   CLASS CATEGORY AGE_GROUP;
   TABLES CATEGORY,
          (AGE_GROUP ALL)*N=" " / RTS=20;
   LABEL AGE_GROUP = 'Age Group'
         CATEGORY = 'LC Category';
   KEYLABEL ALL = 'Combined';
RUN;
```

Just for fun, Program 11-4 uses PROC TABULATE to create a more attractive table than PROC FREQ. In this example, PROC TABULATE uses the keyword ALL to output the sum of the adult and youth counts for each category. If you are not familiar with PROC TABULATE, there are several excellent manuals that can help. In particular, look for *PROC TABULATE by Example*, written by Lauren E. Haworth and published by SAS Publishing. Output from the TABULATE procedure is shown next:

Frequencies of Books by LC Category and Age Group

	Age Group		Combined
	Adult	Youth	
LC Category			
Education	5.00	2.00	7.00
General Works	5.00	1.00	6.00
History	.	2.00	2.00
Literature	7.00	5.00	12.00
Music	11.00	2.00	13.00
Science	13.00	3.00	16.00
Social Sciences	.	3.00	3.00

PROC MEANS and PROC TABULATE are both powerful tools to use in summarizing data. Ideally, the examples in this chapter have given you an appreciation of how useful these data summarizing tools can be.

140

12 Useful Macros

Introduction

This chapter contains a collection of SAS macros that perform several of the longitudinal data tasks described in earlier chapters. This chapter is included primarily for readers who are already familiar with SAS macros. By "packaging" some of the programs described earlier in this book as macros, you can perform some of the common tasks associated with longitudinal data by calling the macro with the appropriate arguments. You may want to use the macros as is, or modify them for your particular needs. For those readers who are unfamiliar with SAS macros, all programming techniques presented in this chapter have already been addressed in earlier chapters, using nonmacro programming.

Listing All or Part of a Data Set

This first example is a very simple macro that lists all or part of a SAS data set, usually for debugging purposes. It is not a macro that is specific to longitudinal data, but I find it so useful, I decided to include it in this chapter. You may think this macro is too short and simple to bother with, but you may find yourself using it all the time. Two features of this macro make it especially useful. First, the macro creates a TITLE statement that includes the data set name. Second, the macro can take a parameter that allows you to print only the first n observations of a data set.

Program 12-1: Creating a Macro to List the Contents of a SAS Data Set

```
*------------------------------------------------------------------*
| Program Name: PRINT.SAS  in C:\LONG\MACROS                       |
| Purpose: Macro which prints out a complete data set or the       |
|          first N observations. The data set name and             |
|          (optionally) the number of observations are included    |
|          in the title.                                           |
| Argument: %PRINT(DSN,OBS=)                                       |
| Examples: %PRINT(TEST,OBS=5)                                     |
|           %PRINT(TEST)                                           |
*------------------------------------------------------------------*;
%MACRO PRINT(DSN,OBS=MAX);
   PROC PRINT DATA=&DSN (OBS=&OBS);
      TITLE "Listing of data set %UPCASE(&DSN)";
      %IF &OBS NE MAX %THEN TITLE2 "First &OBS Observations";;   ❶
   RUN;
%MEND PRINT;
```

Notice that this macro uses both a positional and a named parameter as calling arguments. If you call it with only the data set name, the %IF statement in line ❶ is not true, the default parameter OBS=MAX is used so that the entire data set is printed, and the TITLE2 statement does not execute.

To demonstrate this macro, let's use it to print the first five observations from the CLINICAL data set. You call it like this,

```
%PRINT(CLINICAL,OBS=5);
```

with the following results:

```
Listing of Data Set CLINICAL
First 5 Observations

                  V
                  I
                  S                                           V
                  I                                           I
         P        T   G                                       T
         A        _   E   S                                   A
         T        D   N   T                                   M
    O    E        A   D   A       S   D   D           D   D   I
    b    N        T   E   T   H   B   B   X           X   X   N
    s    T        E   R   E   R   P   P   1           2   3   S

    1  001  21OCT1998  M  NJ  68  130   80  Routine Visit              No
    2  001  11NOV1998  M  NJ  66  132   78  Cold                       No
    3  001  05JAN1999  M  NJ  70  140   88  Cold         Ear Infection No
    4  002  06MAY1999  F  NJ  78  190  100  Ear Infection              Yes
    5  003  04MAR2000  F  NJ  58  108   66  Cold                       Yes
```

Computing Differences between Successive Observations

This next macro takes a SAS data set and creates a new data set containing all the variables in the original data set plus a set of difference variables. These difference variables are the differences from one observation to the next for one or more variables in the variable list. The macro automatically gives a name to each of the difference variables by adding a "D_" prefix to each of the variable names listed in the variable list.

Program 12-2: Creating a Macro to Compute the Differences between Successive Observations in a SAS Data Set

```
*--------------------------------------------------------------*
| Macro Name: DIFF_EVERY_OBS.SAS in  C:\LONG\MACROS            |
| Purpose: Creates a new data set with all the variables in    |
|          the original data set plus the difference between    |
|          the current value and the previous value for all     |
|          variables in the VARLIST.                            |
| Arguments: IN_DSN   = Input data set name                     |
|            OUT_DSN  = Output data set name                     |
|            VARLIST  = List of variables for differences       |
| Example: %DIFF_EVERY_OBS(CLINICAL,NEW,HR SBP DBP)            |
*--------------------------------------------------------------*;
```

```
%MACRO DIFF_EVERY_OBS(IN_DSN,OUT_DSN,VARLIST);
   ***Create a list of variable names to hold the differences and
         add a D_ to the beginning of each variable name;
   %LET TEMP = %STR( &VARLIST);    ❶
   %LET DLIST = %SYSFUNC(TRANWRD(&TEMP,%STR( ),%STR( D_)));    ❷
   DATA &OUT_DSN;
      SET &IN_DSN;
      ARRAY VARS[*] &VARLIST;
      ARRAY DIFF[*] &DLIST;
      DO I = 1 TO DIM(VARS);
         DIFF[I] = DIF(VARS[I]);    ❸
      END;
   DROP I;
%MEND DIFF_EVERY_OBS;
```

First, I would like to thank Russ Tyndall of SAS for his clever way of creating the "D_" variable names. Line ❶ concatenates a blank to the beginning of the variable list. The %SYSFUNC function allows you to use standard DATA step functions and returns the results to the macro processor. The relatively new SAS function called TRANWRD (translate word) substitutes one string for another. For example, the line

```
NEW = TRANWRD(OLD,"RD.","Road");
```

changes all occurrences of "RD." to "Road" in the string OLD, and assigns the resulting string to the variable NEW. In this macro, all the blanks in the VARLIST are replaced by a blank and "D_." So if you had HR SBP DBP as your VARLIST, the macro variable DLIST would be "D_HR D_SBP D_DBP." The only remaining task is to use the DIF function to compute the differences between observations. To demonstrate this macro, we will create a small test data set, call the macro, and use the PRINT macro to list the results.

Program 12-3: Creating a Small Test Data Set and Calling the DIFF_EVERY_OBS Macro

```
DATA TEST;
   INPUT X Y Z;
DATALINES;
1 3 5
2 1 8
5 4 3
9 9 9
;
%DIFF_EVERY_OBS(TEST,OUT,X Y Z);
%PRINT(OUT);
```

The output is shown below:

```
Listing of Data Set OUT

Obs     X     Y     Z     D_X     D_Y     D_Z

 1      1     3     5       .       .       .
 2      2     1     8       1      -2       3
 3      5     4     3       3       3      -5
 4      9     9     9       4       5       6
```

Computing Differences between the First and Last Observations per Subject

This macro is similar to the one above, except that only one observation per subject is written to the output data set, and this observation contains differences between the value of each variable in the VARLIST from the first observation to the last observation (last minus first). Again, the difference variables are created by concatenating a "D_" to each of the variables.

Program 12-4: Creating a Macro to Compute the Differences between the First and Last Observations for Each Subject in a SAS Data Set

```
*-------------------------------------------------------------*
| Macro Name: DIFF_FIRST_LAST.SAS in  C:\LONG\MACROS          |
| Purpose: Using an input data set, creates a new data set    |
|          containing the difference between the first and last|
|          observation for each value of an ID variable, for all|
|          the variables listed in the VARLIST.  The names for |
|          the difference variables will be the names in the   |
|          VARLIST with a "D_" added to the beginning of each name.|
| Arguments: IN_DSN   = Input data set name                   |
|            OUT_DSN  = Output data set name                   |
|            ID_VAR   = ID variable                           |
|            VARLIST  = List of variables for differences      |
| Example: %DIFF_FIRST_LAST(CLINICAL,NEW,PATIENT,HR SBP DBP)  |
*-------------------------------------------------------------*;
```

```
%MACRO DIFF_FIRST_LAST(IN_DSN,OUT_DSN,ID_VAR,VARLIST);
   ***Create a list of variable names to hold the differences;
         add a D_ to the beginning of each variable name;
   %LET TEMP = %STR( &VARLIST);
   %LET DLIST = %SYSFUNC(TRANWRD(&TEMP,%STR( ),%STR( D_)));
   PROC SORT DATA=&IN_DSN OUT=TEMP;
      BY &ID_VAR;
   RUN;

   DATA &OUT_DSN;
      SET &IN_DSN;
      BY &ID_VAR;
      ARRAY VARS[*] &VARLIST;
      ARRAY DIFF[*] &DLIST;
      IF FIRST.&ID_VAR = 1 OR LAST.&ID_VAR = 1 THEN
      DO I = 1 TO DIM(VARS);
         DIFF[I] = DIF(VARS[I]);
      END;
      IF LAST.&ID_VAR = 1 THEN OUTPUT;
      DROP I;
   RUN;

   PROC DATASETS LIBRARY=WORK;
      DELETE TEMP;
   RUN;
%MEND DIFF_FIRST_LAST;
```

The code in this macro is similar to Program 9-3. To demonstrate this macro, we will compute differences in HR and SBP for each PATIENT in the CLINICAL data set. Again, we will use the PRINT macro to list the results.

```
%DIFF_FIRST_LAST(CLINICAL,NEW,PATIENT,HR SBP);
%PRINT(NEW);
```

The output is shown below:

```
Listing of Data Set NEW

                    VISIT_
  Obs   PATIENT      DATE   GENDER  STATE  HR   SBP  DBP  DX1

   1      001     05JAN1999    M     NJ    70   140   88  Cold
   2      002     06MAY1999    F     NJ    78   190  100  Ear Infection
   3      003     12MAY2000    F     NJ    60   110   68  Cold
   4      004     08AUG2000    M     NY    90   180   98  Cold
   5      005     05MAY2000    F     NY    48   110   66  Heart Problem
   6      006     10OCT2000    F     NY    86    .   100  Routine Visit
   7      007     12DEC2000    F     NY     .    .    80  Heart Problem


  Obs          DX2                  DX3        VITAMINS  D_HR   D_SBP

   1    Ear Infection                             No       2     10
   2                                              Yes      8     50
   3                                              Yes      2      2
   4                                              Yes      2    -20
   5    Breathing Problem                         Yes    -42    -70
   6                                              No       0      .
   7    Abdominal Pain       Breathing Problem    Yes      .      .
```

Computing a Moving Average

In Chapter 10 we developed several programs to compute a moving average. The macro presented here creates a new data set with each of the original data points plus a moving average of n data points.

Program 12-5: Creating a Macro to Compute Moving Averages for Every "N" Observations

```
*------------------------------------------------------------------*
| Macro Name: MOVING_AVE in C:\LONG\MACROS                          |
| Purpose: Computes a moving average based on "N" observations      |
| Arguments: IN_DSN    = Data set name                              |
|            OUT_DSN   = Output data set name                       |
|            IN_VAR    = Variable to compute average                |
|            OUT_VAR   = Variable to hold the moving average         |
|            N         = Number of obs for the average              |
| Example: %MOVING_AVE(CLINICAL,TEMP,HR,AVE_HR,5)                   |
*------------------------------------------------------------------*;
%MACRO MOVING_AVE(IN_DSN,OUT_DSN,IN_VAR,OUT_VAR,N);
   DATA &OUT_DSN;
      SET &IN_DSN;
      ***Compute the lags;
      _X1 = &IN_VAR;   ❶
      %DO I = 1 %TO &N;
         %LET NUM = %EVAL(&I + 1);   ❷
          _X&NUM = LAG&I(&IN_VAR);    ❸
      %END;

      ***If the observation number is greater than or equal to the
         number of values needed for the moving average, output;
   IF _N_ GE &N THEN DO;   ❹
      &OUT_VAR = MEAN (OF _X1 - _X&N);   ❺
      OUTPUT;
   END;
   DROP _X: ;   ❻
%MEND MOVING_AVE;
```

This macro creates a set of _Xn variables as temporary placeholders for the LAGn values. _X1 is set equal to the original variable, and the %DO loop creates the family of lagged values. Line ❷ is needed since macro values are normally treated as text values and a function such as the %EVAL function is needed to perform simple arithmetic. For example, in the first iteration of the %DO loop, NUM is equal to 2, and line ❸ reads

```
_X2 = LAG2(&IN_VAR);
```

Once all the lagged values have been computed, the moving average is computed (line ❺) and an observation is written out to the output data set. Although you may have seen it before, the strange-looking DROP statement ❻ uses a colon suffix on the variable name _X. This is a wild-card symbol, and it tells the system to drop all variables that begin with _X.

To try out this macro, let's run it against a small test data set as demonstrated in Program 12-6.

Program 12-6: Creating a Small Test Data Set and Calling the MOVING_AVE Macro

```
DATA TESTAVE;
   INPUT X @@;
DATALINES;
1 3 5 9 9 12 15 20
;
%MOVING_AVE(TESTAVE,TEMP,X,AVE_X,3);
%PRINT(TEMP);
```

The output is shown next:

```
Listing of Data Set TEMP

Obs     X     AVE_X

 1      5     3.0000
 2      9     5.6667
 3      9     7.6667
 4     12    10.0000
 5     15    12.0000
 6     20    15.6667
```

It appears to work as designed. If you don't want to omit the first n -1 observations from the output data set, simply omit line ❹ and the corresponding END statement.

Computing Cell Means and Counts

Even though it is simple enough to use PROC MEANS or PROC SUMMARY to compute cell means (of one or more CLASS variables), the short macro below might be useful if this is a task that you need to do frequently. The macro needs almost no explanation; it is shown in Program 12-7.

Program 12-7: Creating a Macro to Compute Cell Means and Counts

```
*-------------------------------------------------------------------*
| Macro Name: CELLMEANS in C:\LONG\MACROS                           |
| Purpose: Computes means (and n's) for a list of variables,       |
|          given a list of CLASS variables                          |
| Arguments: IN_DSN    = Data set name                              |
|            OUT_DSN   = Output data set name                       |
|            CLASS     = List of CLASS variables                    |
|            VARLIST   = List of variables on which to compute      |
|                        means and counts                           |
| Example: %CELLMEANS(TESTIT,TEMP,GENDER RACE,X Y)                  |
*-------------------------------------------------------------------*;
%MACRO CELLMEANS(IN_DSN, OUT_DSN, CLASS, VARLIST);
   PROC MEANS DATA=&IN_DSN NWAY NOPRINT;
      CLASS &CLASS;
      VAR &VARLIST;
      OUTPUT OUT=&OUT_DSN(DROP = _TYPE_ _FREQ_)
             MEAN= N=/ AUTONAME;
   RUN;
%MEND CELLMEANS;
```

To make this really simple, the AUTONAME output option was used to name the variables holding the cell means and the number of nonmissing values. The sample data set shown in Program 12-8 tests this macro and lists the resulting data set using the PRINT macro.

Program 12-8: Creating a Small Test Data Set and Calling the CELLMEANS Macro

```
DATA TESTIT;
   INPUT RACE $ GENDER $ X Y Z;
DATALINES;
W M 3 4 5
W F 4 5 6
W M 4 5 6
B M 6 5 4
B M 8 7 7
B F 5 4 4
B F 4 2 3
W F 5 4 4
;
%CELLMEANS(TESTIT, TEMP, RACE GENDER, X Y);
%PRINT(TEMP);
```

Output from %PRINT is shown next:

```
Listing of Data Set TEMP

Obs     RACE     GENDER     X_Mean     Y_Mean     X_N     Y_N

 1       B         F          4.5        3.0        2       2
 2       B         M          7.0        6.0        2       2
 3       W         F          4.5        4.5        2       2
 4       W         M          3.5        4.5        2       2
```

Counting the Number of Observations per Subject

Finally, we present a simple macro to count the number of observations for each subject in a longitudinal data set. The result is an output data set containing all the variables of the original input data set plus a count variable. For this macro, we used PROC SQL.

Program 12-9: Creating a Macro to Count the Number of Observations per Subject

```
*-------------------------------------------------------------*
| Macro Name: COUNT_OBS in C:\LONG\MACROS                      |
| Purpose: Counts the number of observations per subject in a  |
|          longitudinal data set                               |
| Arguments: IN_DSN     = Data set name                        |
|            OUT_DSN    = Output data set name                 |
|            IDVAR      = ID Variable                          |
|            COUNTVAR   = Variable to hold the count           |
| Example: %COUNT_OBS (CLINICAL,OUTCLIN, PATIENT, N_VISITS)    |
*-------------------------------------------------------------*;
%MACRO COUNT_OBS(IN_DSN, OUT_DSN, IDVAR, COUNTVAR);
   PROC SQL;
      CREATE TABLE &OUT_DSN AS
      SELECT * ,
         COUNT(&IDVAR) AS &COUNTVAR
      FROM &IN_DSN
      GROUP BY &IDVAR;
   QUIT;
%MEND COUNT_OBS;
```

Calling this macro on the CLINICAL data set, we list the first five observations using the %PRINT macro.

```
%COUNT_OBS(CLINICAL,OUTCLIN,PATIENT,N_VISITS);
%PRINT(OUTCLIN,OBS=5);
```

The listing is shown next:

```
Listing of Data Set OUTCLIN
First 5 Observations


                V                                      V  N
                I                                      I  _
       P        I                                      I  _
       A        T G                                    T  V
       T        _ E S                                  A  I
       I        D N T                                  M  S
 O     E        A D A     S   D   D          D    D    I  I
 b     N        T E T   H B   B   X          X    X    N  T
 s     T        E R E   R P   P   1          2    3    S  S

 1 001 21OCT1998 M NJ 68 130  80 Routine Visit          No 3
 2 001 11NOV1998 M NJ 66 132  78 Cold                   No 3
 3 001 05JAN1999 M NJ 70 140  88 Cold       Ear Infection No 3
 4 002 06MAY1999 F NJ 78 190 100 Ear Infection         Yes 1
 5 003 04MAR2000 F NJ 58 108  66 Cold                  Yes 2
```

The number of visits per patient is now included in the new data set, along with all the original variables.

This chapter demonstrated just a few of the possible macros you may want to keep in your macro library. You can easily turn almost any of the programs presented in this book into a macro by replacing data set names and variable names with the appropriate macro variables.

Appendix List of Data Files and SAS Data Sets

I originally placed all the data-generating programs in each of the appropriate chapters. The comments of several reviewers and some further thought caused me to change my mind and remove the programs from the separate chapters and place them in an appendix. This is the first time I am aware of that someone inserted an appendix rather than removed one. (Sorry for the medical school humor.)

In this appendix, you will find descriptions of SAS data sets used in this book and programs to create them. These programs are available from the companion Web site at www.sas.com/companionsites.

The TEST_SCORES Data Set

Run Program Appendix-1 to create the small student data set. The data set consists of county, school name, teacher name, and three test scores. Each observation represents the scores for one student.

Program Appendix-1: Creating the TEST_SCORES Data Set

```
DATA TEST_SCORES;
   INPUT COUNTY : $9.
         SCHOOL & $21.
         TEACHER : $8.
         MATH
         SCIENCE
         ENGLISH;
DATALINES;
HUNTERDON  FLEMING MIDDLE SCHOOL  SMITH 92 95 88
HUNTERDON  FLEMING MIDDLE SCHOOL  SMITH 94 89 92
```

```
HUNTERDON   FLEMING MIDDLE SCHOOL   SMITH    . 82 84
HUNTERDON   FLEMING MIDDLE SCHOOL   SMITH    .  . 68
HUNTERDON   FLEMING MIDDLE SCHOOL   RIVERA 82 89 72
HUNTERDON   FLEMING MIDDLE SCHOOL   RIVERA 97 94 92
HUNTERDON   FLEMING MIDDLE SCHOOL   RIVERA .  88  .
HUNTERDON   ROBERT HUNTER    GREGORY  80 82 94
HUNTERDON   ROBERT HUNTER    GREGORY  82 84 82
HUNTERDON   ROBERT HUNTER    WRIGHT   60 70 80
HUNTERDON   ROBERT HUNTER    WRIGHT   62 72 83
MIDDLESEX   SAINT BARTS ACADEMY   JONES 72 78 77
MIDDLESEX   SAINT BARTS ACADEMY   JONES 83 83 92
MIDDLESEX   SAINT BARTS ACADEMY   JONES 91 78 81
MIDDLESEX   RUTGERS PREP   MAROTTO . 99  .
MIDDLESEX   RUTGERS PREP   MAROTTO 96 98 98
MIDDLESEX   RUTGERS PREP   MAROTTO 83 88 88
MIDDLESEX   RUTGERS PREP   MAROTTO 84 86 85
MIDDLESEX   RUTGERS PREP   MAROTTO 92 97 93
MIDDLESEX   RUTGERS PREP   FRIEDMAN 99 98 90
MIDDLESEX   RUTGERS PREP   FRIEDMAN 96 95 90
MIDDLESEX   RUTGERS PREP   FRIEDMAN 84 85 84
MIDDLESEX   RUTGERS PREP   PATERSON 68 72 66
MIDDLESEX   RUTGERS PREP   PATERSON 72 74 68
MIDDLESEX   FRANKLIN HIGH   PETERS 80 80 92
MIDDLESEX   FRANKLIN HIGH   PETERS 83 85 88
;
```

A brief word about how the INPUT statement is used in Program Appendix-1 is warranted. The colon (:) and ampersand (&) informat modifiers were used to allow SAS informats to be used with list-directed (separated by spaces) data. The colon modifier says to read the next nonblank value according to the informat supplied. The ampersand modifier works the same way except that the delimiter between the variable being read and the next variable is two or more blanks. In this example, you can read school names that include blanks. Notice that there are two blanks following each of the school names.

The CLINICAL Data Set

The CLINICAL data set represents data from a small (obviously fictitious) clinical practice. Each patient in this sample data set has from one to three visits, each visit being represented by one observation. You will find a patient ID, gender, state code, heart rate, systolic blood pressure, and diastolic blood pressure. Along with these variables, there are three variables to code up to three diagnoses per patient (DX1, DX2, and DX3) and a variable that indicates if the patient is taking vitamins at the time of the visit (VITAMINS). Run Program Appendix-2 to create the CLINICAL data set. If you want, you may include a LIBNAME and two-level data set name and make the data set permanent on your computer.

Program Appendix-2: Creating the CLINICAL Data Set

```
PROC FORMAT;
    VALUE $DXCODE '1' = 'Routine Visit'
                  '2' = 'Cold'
                  '3' = 'Flu'
                  '4' = 'Ear Infection'
                  '5' = 'Heart Problem'
                  '6' = 'Abdominal Pain'
                  '7' = 'Fracture'
                  '8' = 'Breathing Problem'
                  '9' = 'Laceration';
    VALUE $YESNO  '0' = 'No'
                  '1' = 'Yes';
RUN;

DATA CLINICAL;
    INPUT @1  PATIENT     $3.
          @4  VISIT_DATE MMDDYY8.
          @12 GENDER      $1.
          @13 STATE       $2.
          @15 HR          3.
          @18 SBP         3.
          @21 DBP         3.
          @24 (DX1-DX3)   ($1.)
          @27 VITAMINS    $1.;
    FORMAT VISIT_DATE DATE9.
           DX1-DX3     $DXCODE.
           VITAMINS    $YESNO.;
    LABEL PATIENT     = "Patient Number"
          VISIT_DATE = "Visit Date"
          HR          = "Heart Rate"
          SBP         = "Systolic Blood Pressure"
          DBP         = "Diastolic Blood Pressure"
          VITAMINS    = "Is PT Taking Vitamins?";
DATALINES;
00110211998MNJ 68130 801  0
00111111998MNJ 66132 782  0
00101051999MNJ 70140 8824 0
00205061999FNJ 781901004  1
```

```
00303042000FNJ 58108 662   1
00305122000FNJ 60110 682   1
00410301999MNY 8820011079 0
00412121999MNY       1021  1
00408082000MNY 90180 982   1
00505052000FNY 48110 6658 1
00608082000FNY 861841021  1
00610102000FNY 86   1001  0
00712122000FNY       805681
;
PROC SORT DATA=CLINICAL;
   BY PATIENT VISIT_DATE;
RUN;
```

The CLIN_FIRST Data Set

The data set CLIN_FIRST is identical to the data set CLINICAL except that the constant demographic variables (DOB and GENDER) are only entered in the first observation (visit).

Program Appendix-3: Creating the CLIN_FIRST Data Set

```
PROC FORMAT;
    VALUE $DXCODE '1' = 'Routine Visit'
                  '2' = 'Cold'
                  '3' = 'Flu'
                  '4' = 'Ear Infection'
                  '5' = 'Heart Problem'
                  '6' = 'Abdominal Pain'
                  '7' = 'Fracture'
                  '8' = 'Breathing Problem'
                  '9' = 'Laceration';
    VALUE $YESNO  '0' = 'No'
                  '1' = 'Yes';
RUN;


DATA CLIN_FIRST;
    INPUT @1   PATIENT     $3.
          @4   VISIT_DATE  MMDDYY8.
          @12  GENDER      $1.
          @13  STATE       $2.
          @15  HR          3.
          @18  SBP         3.
          @21  DBP         3.
          @24  (DX1-DX3)   ($1.)
```

```
        @27 VITAMINS    $1.;
  FORMAT VISIT_DATE DATE9.
         DX1-DX3     $DXCODE.
         VITAMINS    $YESNO.;
  LABEL PATIENT    = "Patient Number"
        VISIT_DATE = "Visit Date"
        HR         = "Heart Rate"
        SBP        = "Systolic Blood Pressure"
        DBP        = "Diastolic Blood Pressure"
        VITAMINS   = "Is PT Taking Vitamins?";
DATALINES;
00110211998MNJ 68130 801  0
00111111998    66132 782  0
00101051999    70140 8824 0
00205061999FNJ 781901004  1
00303042000FNJ 58108 662  1
00305122000    60110 682  1
00410301999MNY 8820011079 0
00412121999          1021 1
00408082000    90180 982  1
00505052000FNY 48110 6658 1
00608082000FNY 861841021  1
00610102000    86   1001  0
00712122000FNY       805681
;
PROC SORT DATA=CLIN_FIRST;
   BY PATIENT VISIT_DATE;
RUN;
```

The OZONE Data Set

The OZONE data set consists of spore, pollen, ozone, and maximum temperature readings for each of the days from May 1, 1995, to August 31, 1995. Note that this is real data from a monitoring station in New Jersey. Run Program Appendix-4 to create this data set.

Program Appendix-4: Creating the OZONE Data Set

```
DATA OZONE;
    INPUT DATE : MMDDYY10. SPORES POLLEN OZONE MAX_TEMP;
    FORMAT DATE MMDDYY10.;
DATALINES;
05/01/1995 876    2261   36.3   62
05/02/1995 1377   2711   32.0   53
05/03/1995 800    2142   43.7   75
05/04/1995 1421   4029   42.5   71
05/05/1995 1599   6284   33.0   64
05/06/1995 1322   4228   53.6   70
05/07/1995 1322   4109   49.1   71
05/08/1995 1322   4109   39.8   70
05/09/1995 998    1915   43.4   72
05/10/1995 1134   2450   45.3   56
05/11/1995 589    1619   26.4   59
05/12/1995 1545   788    26.2   63
05/13/1995 2397   2642   51.1   75
05/14/1995 2397   2642   33.4   66
05/15/1995 2397   2642   31.8   76
05/16/1995 1565   2291   51.2   82
05/17/1995 6421   4779   34.5   71
05/18/1995 5277   658    29.1   78
05/19/1995 5854   1505   16.7   60
05/20/1995 6430   2352   51.0   79
05/21/1995 6430   2352   68.5   85
05/22/1995 6430   2352   46.5   79
05/23/1995 2152   1874   42.4   77
05/24/1995 2463   1460   71.8   90
05/25/1995 7074   1409   41.2   73
05/26/1995 4256   391    28.5   64
05/27/1995 4283   338    42.9   76
05/28/1995 4310   284    36.1   67
05/29/1995 4310   284    30.3   82
05/30/1995 4310   284    33.6   73
05/31/1995 5630   841    47.7   88
06/01/1995 6462   1096   57.3   86
06/02/1995 3564   697    42.1   80
06/03/1995 4242   477    43.9   85
06/04/1995 4242   477    42.1   82
06/05/1995 4242   477    53.2   85
06/06/1995 8609   415    43.2   81
06/07/1995 2653   75     46.6   91
```

```
06/08/1995 5721   688   60.7   89
06/09/1995 6221   747   39.9   79
06/10/1995 3261   44    31.2   74
06/11/1995 3261   44    41.1   83
06/12/1995 3261   44    29.8   73
06/13/1995 7320   61    24.1   74
06/14/1995 8353   306   20.2   75
06/15/1995 7098   341   42.5   82
06/16/1995 4829   598   62.4   86
06/17/1995 7730   198   72.7   89
06/18/1995 7730   198   87.7   93
06/19/1995 7730   198   94.6   97
06/20/1995 9441   451   81.4   96
06/21/1995 7353   347   33.4   76
06/22/1995 3499   97    29.3   78
06/23/1995 4932   81    23.5   77
06/24/1995 3532   30    26.2   79
06/25/1995 3532   30    31.0   84
06/26/1995 3532   30    39.6   83
06/27/1995 4199   28    26.5   74
06/28/1995 5397   103   29.9   72
06/29/1995 1799   29    34.1   82
06/30/1995 3522   46    41.5   84
07/01/1995 12678  36    35.9   82
07/02/1995 12678  36    32.6   80
07/03/1995 12678  36    48.9   83
07/04/1995 11277  63    72.6   84
07/05/1995 11277  63    53.6   82
07/06/1995 7853   25    45.8   85
07/07/1995 5043   39    27.3   78
07/08/1995 4216   28    70.6   86
07/09/1995 4216   28    24.7   75
07/10/1995 4216   28    51.6   86
07/11/1995 9998   44    61.0   83
07/12/1995 6041   27    70.4   81
07/13/1995 5867   21    77.6   95
07/14/1995 18174  42    94.7   98
07/15/1995 14684  24    102.  104
07/16/1995 14684  24    47.0   87
07/17/1995 14673  24    52.8   86
07/18/1995 6254   14    60.4   90
07/19/1995 24805  24    62.9   88
07/20/1995 11520  34    72.7   88
07/21/1995 17020  39    53.7   84
```

```
07/22/1995 6987    20      81.5    88
07/23/1995 6987    20      60.3    88
07/24/1995 6987    20      62.5    91
07/25/1995 11296   23      65.5    91
07/26/1995 9199    22      52.0    94
07/27/1995 14421   32      74.4    96
07/28/1995 13708   21      55.1    91
07/29/1995 13387   28      58.6    93
07/30/1995 13387   28      56.5    94
07/31/1995 13387   28      60.6    91
;
```

The LIBRARY Data Set

Each observation in the LIBRARY data set corresponds to a single book being checked out of the library. Each record contains an ID, a library name, the current date, and a Library of Congress (LC) number. The ID, library name, and date are entered only in the first record for each patron visit. An LC category is computed from the character part of the LC number, and a due date is computed as the current date plus 14 days. The first character of the ID number also identifies the borrower as adult ("A") or youth ("Y").

Program Appendix-5: Creating the LIBRARY Data Set

```
PROC FORMAT;
    VALUE $CAT 'A'          = 'General Works'
               'B'          = 'Philosophy & Religion'
               'C' - 'F'    = 'History'
               'G'          = 'Geography'
               'H'          = 'Social Sciences'
               'K'          = 'Law'
               'L'          = 'Education'
               'M','ML'     = 'Music'
               'P','PA'-'PT' = 'Literature'
               'Q'          = 'Science'
               'R'          = 'Medicine'
               'T'          = 'Technology';
    VALUE DAYWK 1 = 'Sun.'  2 = 'Mon.'  3 = 'Tue.'  4 = 'Wed.'
                5 = 'Thu.'  6 = 'Fri.'  7 = 'Sat.';
    VALUE $AGEGRP 'A' = 'Adult'
                  'Y' = 'Youth';
RUN;
```

```
DATA LIBRARY;
    INPUT @1   ID        $5.
          @6   LIBRARY   $10.
          @16  DATE      MMDDYY8.
          @24  LC        $10.;
    LENGTH CATEGORY $ 25;

    ***Extract the LC category: 1- or 2-characters before first digit;
    FIRST_N = INDEXC(LC,'0123456789'); ***Position of first numeral;
    CATEGORY = PUT(SUBSTR(LC,1,FIRST_N - 1),$CAT.);

    ***LIBRARY name and DATE are only entered on the first record for
       each visit.;
    ***Copy Library information from the first non-blank entry if blank;
    LENGTH HOLD_LIB $ 10 AGE_GROUP $ 1;
    RETAIN HOLD_LIB HOLD_DATE;

    IF LIBRARY NE " " THEN DO;
       HOLD_LIB = LIBRARY;
       HOLD_DATE = DATE;
    END;

    ELSE DO;
       LIBRARY = HOLD_LIB;
       DATE = HOLD_DATE;
    END;

    DUE_DATE = DATE + 14;
    DAY = WEEKDAY(DATE);
    AGE_GROUP = SUBSTR(ID,1,1);

    FORMAT DATE DUE_DATE DATE9. DAY DAYWK. AGE_GROUP $AGEGRP.;
    DROP HOLD_: FIRST_N;
DATALINES;
Y0123CLINTON    10212000H410.B5
Y0123                  H415.A7
A1234FLEMINGTON10212000Q550.B10
A1234                  Q550.C8
A1234                  M410.C12
A2121CLINTON    10212000PA317.A9
Y8888FLEMINGTON10212000E110.A1
Y8888                  F441.B9
A7654FLEMINGTON10212000ML440.B5
```

```
A8765CLINTON      10212000L550.V5
A8765                  L550.D3
A8765                  L550.E3
A8765                  L551.A6
Y6565FLEMINGTON10232000Q220.B7
Y6565                  Q220.C7
A1022CLINTON      10232000Q660.A12
A1022                  Q660.B3
A1022                  Q450.C4
A2888CLINTON      10232000ML120.S22
A3433CLINTON      10232000A1200.D7
A1010FLEMINGTON10232000PN450.A1
A1010                  PN555.V8
A1010                  PA380.C1
A1010                  P555.C8
Y2033FLEMINGTON10232000ML233.D3
Y2033                  M330.C8
A2345CLINTON      10242000Q22.C1
A2345                  Q23.F66
Y0123CLINTON      10252000H415.D22
A9545FLEMINGTON10252000A433.B8
A9545                  A450.S2
A6198CLINTON      10252000M766.D71
A7734CLINTON      10252000Q552.B88
A7734                  Q455.A1
Y6644FLEMINGTON10262000P555.C43
A3344FLEMINGTON10272000M233.C5
A3344                  M233.D1
A3344                  ML400.C8
A1234CLINTON      10282000M550.V77
A1234                  Q440.B22
A1234                  Q440.F34
Y1322FLEMINGTON10302000P1200.V7
Y1322                  P890.E4
Y1322                  PA220.G8
A9988CLINTON      10302000M733.C3
A1747FLEMINGTON10300000L7.D8
Y0011FLEMINGTON10312000L345.F76
Y0011                  L299.A3
A4949CLINTON      10312000PA444.B88
A4949                  PA444.B9
A2121CLINTON      11012000A3345.X77
A2121                  A300.V6
Y2345FLEMINGTON11012000Q33.A44
```

```
Y4433FLEMINGTON11012000A878.B81
A4444CLINTON   11022000M888.B9
A4444              ML500.V7
Y0123FLEMINGTON11042000PA970.V4
A2121CLINTON   11062000Q355.B8
A2121              Q355.V44
;
```

Index

Books Available from SAS® Press

Advanced Log-Linear Models Using SAS®
by **Daniel Zelterman**

Analysis of Clinical Trials Using SAS®: A Practical Guide
by **Alex Dmitrienko, Geert Molenberghs, Walter Offen,** and **Christy Chuang-Stein**

Analyzing Receiver Operating Characteristic Curves with SAS®
by **Mithat Gönen**

Annotate: Simply the Basics
by **Art Carpenter**

Applied Multivariate Statistics with SAS® Software, Second Edition
by **Ravindra Khattree** and **Dayanand N. Naik**

Applied Statistics and the SAS® Programming Language, Fifth Edition
by **Ronald P. Cody** and **Jeffrey K. Smith**

An Array of Challenges — Test Your SAS® Skills
by **Robert Virgile**

Basic Statistics Using SAS® Enterprise Guide®: A Primer
by **Geoff Der** and **Brian S. Everitt**

Building Web Applications with SAS/IntrNet®: A Guide to the Application Dispatcher
by **Don Henderson**

Carpenter's Complete Guide to the SAS® Macro Language, Second Edition
by **Art Carpenter**

Carpenter's Complete Guide to the SAS® REPORT Procedure
by **Art Carpenter**

The Cartoon Guide to Statistics
by **Larry Gonick** and **Woollcott Smith**

Categorical Data Analysis Using the SAS® System, Second Edition
by **Maura E. Stokes, Charles S. Davis,** and **Gary G. Koch**

Cody's Data Cleaning Techniques Using SAS®, Second Edition
by **Ron Cody**

Common Statistical Methods for Clinical Research with SAS® Examples, Second Edition
by **Glenn A. Walker**

The Complete Guide to SAS® Indexes
by **Michael A. Raithel**

CRM Segmemtation and Clustering Using SAS® Enterprise Miner™
by **Randall S. Collica**

Data Management and Reporting Made Easy with SAS® Learning Edition 2.0
by **Sunil K. Gupta**

Data Preparation for Analytics Using SAS®
by **Gerhard Svolba**

Debugging SAS® Programs: A Handbook of Tools and Techniques
by **Michele M. Burlew**

support.sas.com/publishing

Decision Trees for Business Intelligence and Data Mining: Using SAS® Enterprise Miner™
by **Barry de Ville**

Efficiency: Improving the Performance of Your SAS® Applications
by **Robert Virgile**

Elementary Statistics Using JMP®
by **Sandra D. Schlotzhauer**

The Essential Guide to SAS® Dates and Times
by **Derek P. Morgan**

Fixed Effects Regression Methods for Longitudinal Data Using SAS®
by **Paul D. Allison**

Genetic Analysis of Complex Traits Using SAS®
by **Arnold M. Saxton**

The Global English Style Guide: Writing Clear, Translatable Documentation for a Global Market
by **John R. Kohl**

A Handbook of Statistical Analyses Using SAS®, Second Edition
by **B.S. Everitt**
and **G. Der**

Health Care Data and SAS®
by **Marge Scerbo, Craig Dickstein,**
and **Alan Wilson**

The How-To Book for SAS/GRAPH® Software
by **Thomas Miron**

In the Know... SAS® Tips and Techniques From Around the Globe, Second Edition
by **Phil Mason**

Instant ODS: Style Templates for the Output Delivery System
by **Bernadette Johnson**

Integrating Results through Meta-Analytic Review Using SAS® Software
by **Morgan C. Wang**
and **Brad J. Bushman**

Introduction to Data Mining Using SAS® Enterprise Miner™
by **Patricia B. Cerrito**

Introduction to Design of Experiments with JMP® Examples, Third Edition
by **Jacques Goupy**
and **Lee Creighton**

JMP® for Basic Univariate and Multivariate Statistics: A Step-by-Step Guide
by **Ann Lehman, Norm O'Rourke, Larry Hatcher,**
and **Edward J. Stepanski**

JMP® Start Statistics: A Guide to Statistics and Data Analysis Using JMP®, Fourth Edition
by **John Sall, Lee Creighton,**
and **Ann Lehman**

Learning SAS® by Example: A Programmer's Guide
by **Ron Cody**

The Little SAS® Book: A Primer
by **Lora D. Delwiche**
and **Susan J. Slaughter**

The Little SAS® Book: A Primer, Second Edition
by **Lora D. Delwiche**
and **Susan J. Slaughter**
(updated to include SAS 7 features)

The Little SAS® Book: A Primer, Third Edition
by **Lora D. Delwiche**
and **Susan J. Slaughter**
(updated to include SAS 9.1 features)

The Little SAS® Book: A Primer, Fourth Edition
by **Lora D. Delwiche**
and **Susan J. Slaughter**
(updated to include SAS 9.2 features)

The Little SAS® Book for Enterprise Guide® 3.0
by **Susan J. Slaughter**
and **Lora D. Delwiche**

support.sas.com/publishing

The Little SAS® Book for Enterprise Guide® 4.1
by **Susan J. Slaughter**
and **Lora D. Delwiche**

Logistic Regression Using the SAS® System:
Theory and Application
by **Paul D. Allison**

Longitudinal Data and SAS®: A Programmer's Guide
by **Ron Cody**

Maps Made Easy Using SAS®
by **Mike Zdeb**

Measurement, Analysis, and Control Using JMP®: Quality
Techniques for Manufacturing
by **Jack E. Reece**

Multiple Comparisons and Multiple Tests Using
SAS® Text and Workbook Set
(books in this set also sold separately)
by **Peter H. Westfall, Randall D. Tobias,
Dror Rom, Russell D. Wolfinger,**
and **Yosef Hochberg**

Multiple-Plot Displays: Simplified with Macros
by **Perry Watts**

Multivariate Data Reduction and Discrimination with
SAS® Software
by **Ravindra Khattree**
and **Dayanand N. Naik**

Output Delivery System: The Basics
by **Lauren E. Haworth**

Painless Windows: A Handbook for SAS® Users,
Third Edition
by **Jodie Gilmore**
(updated to include SAS 8 and SAS 9.1 features)

Pharmaceutical Statistics Using SAS®:
A Practical Guide
Edited by **Alex Dmitrienko, Christy Chuang-Stein,**
and **Ralph D'Agostino**

The Power of PROC FORMAT
by **Jonas V. Bilenas**

Predictive Modeling with SAS® Enterprise Miner™:
Practical Solutions for Business Applications
by **Kattamuri S. Sarma**

PROC SQL: Beyond the Basics Using SAS®
by **Kirk Paul Lafler**

PROC SQL by Example: Using SQL within SAS®
by **Howard Schreier**

PROC TABULATE by Example
by **Lauren E. Haworth**

Professional SAS® Programmer's Pocket Reference,
Fifth Edition
by **Rick Aster**

Professional SAS® Programming Shortcuts,
Second Edition
by **Rick Aster**

Quick Results with SAS/GRAPH® Software
by **Arthur L. Carpenter**
and **Charles E. Shipp**

Quick Results with the Output Delivery System
by **Sunil Gupta**

Reading External Data Files Using SAS®: Examples
Handbook
by **Michele M. Burlew**

Regression and ANOVA: An Integrated Approach
Using SAS® Software
by **Keith E. Muller**
and **Bethel A. Fetterman**

Regression Using JMP®
by **Rudolf J. Freund, Ramon C. Littell,**
and **Lee Creighton**

SAS® For Dummies®
by **Stephen McDaniel**
and **Chris Hemedinger**

SAS® for Forecasting Time Series, Second Edition
by **John C. Brocklebank**
and **David A. Dickey**

support.sas.com/publishing

SAS® for Linear Models, Fourth Edition
by **Ramon C. Littell, Walter W. Stroup,**
and **Rudolf Freund**

SAS® for Mixed Models, Second Edition
by **Ramon C. Littell, George A. Milliken, Walter W. Stroup,**
Russell D. Wolfinger, and **Oliver Schabenberger**

SAS® for Monte Carlo Studies: A Guide for Quantitative
Researchers
by **Xitao Fan, Ákos Felsővályi, Stephen A. Sivo,**
and **Sean C. Keenan**

SAS® Functions by Example
by **Ron Cody**

SAS® Graphics for Java: Examples Using SAS® AppDev
Studio™ and the Output Delivery System
by **Wendy Bohnenkamp**
and **Jackie Iverson**

SAS® Guide to Report Writing, Second Edition
by **Michele M. Burlew**

SAS® Macro Programming Made Easy,
Second Edition
by **Michele M. Burlew**

SAS® Programming by Example
by **Ron Cody**
and **Ray Pass**

SAS® Programming for Enterprise Guide® Users
by **Neil Constable**

SAS® Programming in the Pharmaceutical Industry
by **Jack Shostak**

SAS® Survival Analysis Techniques for Medical Research,
Second Edition
by **Alan B. Cantor**

SAS® System for Elementary Statistical Analysis,
Second Edition
by **Sandra D. Schlotzhauer**
and **Ramon C. Littell**

SAS® System for Regression, Third Edition
by **Rudolf J. Freund**
and **Ramon C. Littell**

SAS® System for Statistical Graphics, First Edition
by **Michael Friendly**

The SAS® Workbook and Solutions Set
(books in this set also sold separately)
by **Ron Cody**

Saving Time and Money Using SAS®
by **Philip R. Holland**

Selecting Statistical Techniques for Social Science
Data: A Guide for SAS® Users
by **Frank M. Andrews, Laura Klem, Patrick M.**
O'Malley, Willard L. Rodgers, Kathleen B. Welch,
and **Terrence N. Davidson**

Statistics Using SAS® Enterprise Guide®
by **James B. Davis**

A Step-by-Step Approach to Using the SAS® System
for Factor Analysis and Structural Equation Modeling
by **Larry Hatcher**

A Step-by-Step Approach to Using SAS®
for Univariate and Multivariate Statistics,
Second Edition
by **Norm O'Rourke, Larry Hatcher,**
and **Edward J. Stepanski**

Step-by-Step Basic Statistics Using SAS®: Student
Guide and Exercises
(books in this set also sold separately)
by **Larry Hatcher**

Survival Analysis Using SAS®:
A Practical Guide
by **Paul D. Allison**

Tuning SAS® Applications in the OS/390 and z/OS
Environments, Second Edition
by **Michael A. Raithel**

Using SAS® in Financial Research
by **Ekkehart Boehmer, John Paul Broussard,**
and **Juha-Pekka Kallunki**

Validating Clinical Trial Data Reporting with SAS®
by **Carol I. Matthews**
and **Brian C. Shilling**

support.sas.com/publishing

Visualizing Categorical Data
by **Michael Friendly**

Web Development with SAS® by Example, Second Edition
by **Frederick E. Pratter**

Example Code — Examples from This Book at Your Fingertips

You can access the example programs for this book by linking to its companion Web site at **support.sas.com/companionsites**. Select the book title to display its companion Web site, and select **Example Code and Data** to display the SAS programs that are included in the book.

For an alphabetical listing of all books for which example code is available, see **support.sas.com/bookcode**. Select a title to display the book's example code.

If you are unable to access the code through the Web site, send e-mail to **saspress@sas.com**.

Comments or Questions?

If you have comments or questions about this book, you may contact the author through SAS as follows.

Mail: SAS Institute Inc.
SAS Press
Attn: <Author's name>
SAS Campus Drive
Cary, NC 27513

E-mail: saspress@sas.com

Fax: (919) 677-4444

Please include the title of the book in your correspondence.

See the last pages of this book for a complete list of books available through **SAS Press** or visit **support.sas.com/publishing**.

SAS Publishing News: Receive up-to-date information about all new SAS publications via e-mail by subscribing to the SAS Publishing News monthly eNewsletter. Visit **support.sas.com/subscribe**.